To my friend Betty —

Always look for rainbows!

C.J. Morgan

(the Roselady, 2010)

AF544651

Roselady

A Story of Hope, Change and Perseverance

By C.J. Morgan

Roselady
© 2008 by C.J. Morgan
All rights reserved. No portion of this book may be reproduced in any fashion, either mechanically or electronically, without the express written permission of the author. Short excerpts may be used with the permission of the author or the publisher for the purpose of media reviews.

Second edition, January 2009
Printed in the United States of America
ISBN 978-0-9819325-4-5

Published by Top Ten Productions, Inc.
615-289-4815

Cover Photography; Steve Ellis, Light House Studio
Cover design; Tom Walker, Sevierville, TN
Interior Book design; Kimberly Martin

Dedication

This book is dedicated to my son Brian, who ultimately lived most of the journey with me. Having him changed the direction of my life, offered me that most holy and gracious opportunity of being a mother and taught me to love. It is also dedicated to my wonderful nephew, Richard, of whom I am very proud and to my very special grandson, Mason, who is barely starting out on his own journey.
I hope it is a long and happy one.

Acknowledgments

I would like to thank God, my family (with a special note of thanks to Mom and Dad), Bob and Jean Johnson, Joe Don Scoggins, Rachelle, Jo Ann, Penny, Diana, Darrell, Rita, Ida Gay, Bon, Carole Ann, Nora, Bonnie Kate, Ruby Walton, Larry and Doris and others who read early drafts and gave me the courage to keep on writing, Tom and Lou Ann Walker, Anne Whitworth, Dr. Chironna and the Patricia Neal Rehabilitation Center, Lisa Corcoran of Corcoran & Nelli LLC, Gayle Cantrell from Lightning Source, the Ella Lyman Cabot Trust, all my friends on the rose route, my UAW-Ford family, the residents of Kirby Pines Retirement Community in Memphis, Tenn., my friends at Renaissance Terrace Assisted Living in Knoxville, TN, professors at the University of Utah and the University of Tennessee, Kimberly Martin of Self-Pub.net, clients, customers, students, audiences and those who have supported me and shown kindness in so many ways throughout the years.

You know who you are.

Roselady

Authors note;

During my recovery from a head injury, I was asked to speak to several groups. Audience members told me I should write a book, that I'd had experiences and have an outlook that could be of benefit to others. My feeling is that *everyone* has a book inside them – we all have interesting and unique stories and lives, and I wasn't in any hurry to share mine.

As time went on, however, I became too busy to accept speaking engagements so I thought perhaps a book could speak for me. Eventually I began the outlining process and making notes. But I found that I couldn't write about a life-changing event without writing about the life itself. I also realized that there had been *many* life-changing events - not just one. Some were big and some were small but I learned something from each of them. And, I knew that if a book were to help anyone, it would have to be honest.

I found that being honest with oneself may be one of the hardest things for any human being to do. Facing reality and dealing with it in a positive sense are points of personal progress that are never achieved by many.

We often prefer to keep unpleasantness and even confusion cloaked behind a veil of secrecy, but until we generate dialog within our own frame of reference as well as the larger culture, the unpleasantness will continue. We will just keep repeating our mistakes over and over again.

We cannot address social ills like domestic abuse, addictions, war and crime, as well as personal issues that cause turbulence and anxiety without bringing them out into the open.

Pretending that everything is perfect in an imperfect world won't make anything better. Frank, open discussion is a first step toward awareness and remedy.

The writing of the book was a cathartic experience, in that sense.

As I wrote about my husband's battle with Post-Traumatic Stress Disorder, my heart was with those who are returning from the Middle East with similar battle scars. I want to believe that my husband's problems helped pave the way for them to get the assistance they might need.

In writing about my brother's illness and later during my own battle with Traumatic Brain Injury, I hoped that as a society, we can realize that not all handicaps are visible and learn not to be judgmental of those who may be different.

In writing about my life, I realized that I had fallen into a trap, making the same wrong-headed, codependent choices in some areas. I also realized that in many ways, I had not taken personal responsibility for who I was - and what I was. (As adults, we have a say in this.) But I can choose to break those patterns or continue, with the knowledge that *if you do what you've always done, you'll get what you've always gotten.* I can recognize and accept my own reality.

I have offered facts, not a fairy tale. Some names have been changed to respect privacy. Old clippings, records, contracts, letters, bills and other artifacts can verify dates, locations and truth. The manuscript was read by many of the individuals involved, or those who could bear witness and was checked for accuracy, where my own facts or memory may have been inadequate or distorted.

With regard to Traumatic Brain Injury, my message remains one of prevention. Readers can draw their own conclusions about how I was before the head injury and how I was after. It is important to note that my symptoms, reactions and path to recovery might not be the same as for others. My life philosophy may be different as well.

Readers can embrace my interpretation of events or develop their own. I have left out a great deal because it would be impossible to include everything. We are left with a general sense of how things were and a broad brushstroke instead of a definite direction. But it is my hope that by sharing my memories and my life so far, I will have helped *someone* - which was the original plan.

C.J. Morgan, 2008

Contents

Part 3 - Tennessee

Part 4 - Nashville

Roselady

A Story of Hope, Change and Perseverance

By C.J. Morgan

And now I'm glad I didn't know
The way it all would end the way it all would go
Our lives are better left to chance
I could have missed the pain
But I'd have had to miss the dance

- The Dance, Garth Brooks

Prologue

How does a talented, spirited, college-educated mother of one, who was once on her way to a challenging, fast-track professional career, find herself broke, homeless, alone and sleeping in her car at a Wal-Mart parking lot??

The last thing I remembered at the club was a crash, a blinding flash of white light, then nothing.

The next thing I knew, a woman was in my face yelling at me to "Wake up but DON'T MOVE!!"

Sprawled and immobile on the floor, I vaguely remembered where I was. I didn't know what happened but was concerned about whether or not I had worn underwear beneath my party dress that evening.

Lying there for what seemed like a long time, fading between reality and unconsciousness, I was only dimly aware of the crowd and loud music, which somehow seemed very far away. I wondered why the woman kneeling at my side kept yelling.

As the designated driver for my sister-in-law and a few other friends, we had been celebrating someone's birthday at a local nightclub. A wall mounted television set had fallen on my head, the force of the impact knocking me backward, off the stool and onto the floor, unconscious.

Paramedics came and as they wheeled me out, my friends followed. They in turn were followed by the staff of the establishment, who wanted to make sure our bill was paid.

At the emergency room I was conscious, but I don't remember what was X-rayed. A huge lump had formed on the right half of my forehead near the hairline and the back of my head was sore from hitting the floor but apparently no bones were broken and there was no blood, so they sent me home. As we were leaving, the attending physician said I might have a concussion and to watch for weird or unusual behavior.

"How will we know the difference?" cracked my dear, whiskey-voiced, smart-ass sister-in-law.

Part 1
Wisconsin

Chapter 1

Childhood; teaching my dolls

Down that hillbilly highway, that hillbilly highway
Hillbilly highway goes on and on.

- Hillbilly Highway, Steve Earle

In 1959, there were not freeways, just narrow two-lane roads winding through the mountains of Kentucky and East Tennessee. The towns of Corbin, Jellico, and Cumberland Gap stood like aged soldiers standing sentinel between stretches of wilderness. Each one featured weathered old men in front of dusty-looking storefronts with tin signs and legions of dogs that ran loose or sat quietly on porches.

There were hillbilly gift shops featuring so-called Indian trinkets made of plastic, stamped "Made in Japan." There were Texaco stations and 24-hour diners with gravel parking lots and tired-looking customers. Ramshackle dwellings perched at the side of the road, their yards cluttered by yesterday's treasures, unused appliances and assorted, rusted auto parts.

This was the route we took almost yearly from where I was born in Southern Wisconsin to where my father was born in East Tennessee.

We sometimes made the trip in 12 hours, driving straight through. In the dark, I was hypnotized for miles by the faint glow of red taillights from the cars ahead of us.

When we drove all night, I felt it my duty to keep up a constant chatter in Daddy's ear so he wouldn't fall asleep. In those days, I could stand in the backseat and rest my head on his shoulder as he drove, or stand in the front seat beside him. Unfettered by seat belts, our world was illuminated by the dull, greenish glow of the dashboard lights. My mother and little brother slept, and sometimes I grew sleepy and quiet as well. Occasionally Daddy would turn the radio on, breaking the silence. As he turned the dials in search of a far-off country music station, we listened until there was more static than music.

Sometimes we stopped for snacks or a soda – or to go to the restroom. On the road again during daylight hours, there were places where this 5-year-old girl could look out the car window straight down into deep gorges, riding on the edge of a cliff it seemed. With little or no shoulder on the side of the road, I hoped and prayed fervently that the car wouldn't slide into the abyss.

In spite of a nervous but implicit trust in my father's driving ability, sometimes I was so terrified, I slid down onto the floor in the backseat so I couldn't see the bluffs, deep valleys, and purple rise of the Appalachian scenery.

I don't remember what year Daddy told me those were "friendly" mountains, but I grew to love them, as I loved my father's people and I began to eagerly look forward to these trips.

As we traveled, the gentle Southern accent of a waitress or cashier, usually somewhere in Indiana, signaled for me a change in the cultural climate and triggered a sense of escape. The mountains of East Tennessee became a refuge of hope and peace for me over the years, a quiet voice telling me that all was well.

Those two-lane curves have given way to four-lane interstates now. The 24-hour diners have become mega-truck stops, blazing in the night with enough lights for a small city. The mom and pop hotels and gas stations have become dilapidated shadows of what used to be, but even today I am enveloped in serenity within those mountains and feel that I have come home at last.

Albion, Wis., where I spent my earliest years, was a village of a few hundred people in the mid-1950s. I remember two tiny stores that sold penny candy, a town hall, a church and the park with a historic cannon on display, where my brother and I used to play.

It was a time when no one locked doors, teenagers rode by on their bikes and Cracker Jacks still had good prizes. Mama made scrapes and bruises better with a kiss, and the sounds of my childhood included crickets, birds and barking dogs.

My very first love was "Ta-ta," my maternal great-grandfather. Great Grandpa McCarthy, with his tufts of white hair and wild, bushy eyebrows, had other grandchildren, but you wouldn't have known it from the way he spoiled me.

Ta-ta drove on the wrong side of the road, parked on the curb and played a mean tuba until he no longer had enough lung power. I toddled three steps behind him, through the huge vegetable garden, clutching Bimbo, my precious, battered, rubber doll.

Great Grandma McCarthy, with her kind eyes, gentle smile and carefully-coifed gray hair was always cooking or baking something and was seldom seen without an apron.

When I grew older, I would climb onto the round piano stool to reach the ancient upright keyboard at their house and hammer out simple, one-fingered tunes, eventually adding more fingers. Sometimes someone would request that I perform, then offer applause and praise, which I accepted with a humble, beaming smile and something I recognized as totally false modesty, even at age 3.

At 4, I was given dance lessons, which didn't stick. Even then, I didn't like rehearsing. During a recital, I stopped mid-performance to see what the other dancers were doing, obviously lost. It's a good thing parents weren't armed with video cameras back then. Never good at synchronized choreography, I did eventually prove to be adept at free-form modern dance and clogging. I had rhythm.

My favorite parts of dance class and recitals were the costumes, especially the little polka-dot satin and tulle tutu. I kept it for many years and would wear it at the drop of a hat, no matter how inappropriate the occasion, until it no longer fit.

I loved to dress up and was very good at pretending. I could pretend I was a ballerina. Or a princess. Or a cowgirl. Or anything I could imagine being.

At age 6, I pretended I was a bride. Dressed in a white veil and with other family members in attendance, I solemnly "married" Mike Monday, age 7. My somewhat reluctant groom had other duties, though, and soon went off to play army with the other boys.

My Saturday morning television heroes and earliest girlhood crushes, (other than Mike Monday) were Sky King, who thwarted bad guys and found lost hikers from the cockpit of his twin engine Cessna, and Mighty Mouse, a handsome, virile flying mouse, a la Superman.

Later, Marshall Matt Dillon from *Gunsmoke* and Adam Cartright from *Bonanza,* both popular westerns, fanned the flames of my vague girlish desires.

I was an inquisitive child and sometimes got a lot of attention because I was also rather sickly. Because of my chronic asthma, bronchitis and ear infections, Dr. Neeno made house calls regularly, back when doctors still did such a thing.

When I was a child, Daddy wasn't home often. He worked very hard as a truck driver and was gone a lot, but I felt loved and special most of the time.

My mantra, as he left for work, was a singsong "Bye Dad. Don't have a wreck, but if you do, don't get hurt!" Part prayer and part superstition, I believed that by uttering these words aloud with him in hearing distance, he was protected from harm and it bothered me when I didn't get to bless his departure with them.

Upon Dad's return, my younger brother Clark, Mom, and I would run to the door to greet him. Normally fastidious and tidy in grooming and appearance, Dad might now be covered with dirt or grease saying "Don't come near me, I smell like a buffalo!" but we didn't care.

At age 6, I had never smelled a buffalo, but it wouldn't have mattered. He was Daddy and it didn't matter what he smelled like. It is interesting, though, that I still like men who smell like a combination of diesel fuel, cigarettes and Jade East cologne.

When Clark and I were very young, Dad once said he was going to Cedar Rapids, a town in Iowa. Misunderstanding him, of course, we wanted to "see the rabbits" too!

Another time, we overheard a telephone conversation between Mom and Dad. Hearing only Mother's end of the conversation, we heard that Dad was *tied up* somewhere!

Our imaginations ran wild with wide-eyed visions of our father bound to a tree with ropes by primitive hostile natives, like on television!

Mother tried to keep us occupied and entertained while Dad was gone but sometimes she would hurriedly pack our bags, herd us into the car, get into the driver's seat and we would all follow behind his big car hauler. Company regulations wouldn't allow us to ride in the truck with him.

Around a curve, he would stick his tanned arm out the window and wave to us as the miles went by. The Midwestern scenery unfolded before us, the windows down and the sound of his truck ahead. We watched him unload the cars one by one at dealerships; then it was back to the two-lane highway again.

We stayed at cheap roadside cottages that smelled of mold and dust, but these spontaneous adventures were fun and exciting. These trips both fueled and satisfied the sense of restlessness already in my soul and I could hear the distant call of those friendly mountains in Tennessee.

Sometimes when Dad was gone, my then stay-at-home mom would take us to the movies. I was terrified of Sleeping Beauty's archenemy: Maleficent. To me, the swirling black and purple cloak she wore and the gaseous green clouds surrounding her embodied pure evil. While she was on-screen, I hid on the floor behind the seat in front of me.

As afraid as I was of Maleficent, I was totally enchanted with Secret Agent Matt Helm, played by entertainer Dean Martin, and his bevy of beauties. Agent Helm was a James Bond-type character but funnier, breezier and infinitely sexier, although I didn't really know what that meant, at the time.

Mom also took us to the local wading pools in the parks and the zoo, the lake, the state capital, and the old red and white McDonald's that kept track of how many burgers had been served. I had visions of an employee counting each order as it went out.

"Who keeps track?" I once asked Mom.

"Of what?"

"The hamburgers…"

"They probably keep an inventory," She replied.

"What's an inventory?" I asked.

She sighed. "A record of everything."

"How do they do that?" I wondered aloud.

I was full of questions about everything, and although Mother had graduated from high school, she was hard pressed to answer them all.

Mama was pretty and smart and she spoiled me tremendously, as did all the other relatives, although I think Mom sometimes felt a bit overwhelmed with life and responsibilities. This was evidenced by her frequent slides into depression, often involving retreating to her room for days on end and staying in tears for weeks at a time.

Sitting on the floor, surrounded by stacks of unread newspapers and unable to function, she must have been frustrated, with no personal outlets or social life, raising two children essentially alone. I remember going to stay with Papa and Memo, my maternal grandparents, while Mommy went away for a while.

Papa and Memo were indulgent and supportive - my biggest fans. At their house, there were campfires and weenie roasts, Easter egg hunts in the parlor, and a junk drawer stocked with household treasures designed to delight visiting grandchildren.

I inherited Memo's love of writing and her fondness for cats along with Papa's sense of humor and mischief. They always made a fuss over me, planting a seed of confidence, imparting a sense of family and providing a tiny oasis of consistency.

Throughout the years, I played in their big yard and later explored the nearby creek for hours with my brother and cousins. But, as I picked dandelions on their front lawn at age 4, I didn't know that my hospitalized mother was battling demons of depression that my father didn't believe existed.

My strong-minded father was an independent thinker who had overcome much and believed others could as well. He brought Mom home from the hospital, having little patience with illness of any kind back then, and flushed her medication down the drain. He said she didn't need the pills; it was "all in her head," which, of course, is where all forms of mental illness reside.

To be fair, he asked a pharmacist's opinion first, but a druggist may not have been the best person to call the shots. Of course, nobody knew very much about depression - or other forms of mental illness - at that time.

At home again, Mom did her best to try to deal with daily life.

My brother and I just thought her bobby pins were in too tight.

Going to Papa and Memo's house was a welcome respite from turmoil at home. When feelings run deep, tempers sometimes flare. Mom and Dad had "wars with words," as Dad puts it. Arguments between them hung in the air for hours afterward but there was often genuine affection between them. Their embraces in the kitchen throughout the years, sometimes followed by a playful pat on Mom's rear end from Dad were so commonplace that eventually both their tiny grandsons took to patting their Grandma's behind, thinking it was the thing to do.

But Dad could just as easily provoke Mom's fury and fuel a downward spiral. Her mood often seemed to depend on his and sometimes it was Dad who became emotionally overwrought. As my brother and I grew older, we were both subjected to his occasional temper and short fuse.

We both recall lying in our beds alone, hearing raised voices, cursing and the sounds of what often sounded like furniture being thrown coming from our parents' bedroom or the living room.

Later, after developing an attitude and temper of my own, I would stand up to Dad, resulting in bruises on both of us. He was always sorry later and of course I was too. Mother, who hated violence of any kind, became an emotional wreck during these brawls, staying mad at both of us.

Ghosts from their own childhoods, pressure and responsibility added up to stress in my parents' relationship but as a kid, I didn't know anything was amiss. I thought my childhood was normal and everyone lived like this.

Like many other families, we had our ups and downs but we were close.

One of the landmarks in Albion was the church. This was a Seventh-Day Baptist church that my mother's extended family attended. Each year, children took part in a Christmas program where everyone read a Bible verse or poem in front of a giant Christmas tree. Being honestly materialistic, as far as I was concerned, the real fun began afterward when presents were distributed from under the tree for every child. I waited impatiently each year for my bounty.

The church basement was often the site of festivities, luncheons and celebrations, and the church was the social and civic heart of the community. However, the first wedding I remember attending was when my second cousin Carole Ann got married at a Catholic church in nearby Edgerton.

She looked like my angelic bride doll and was beautiful walking down the aisle in her white gown. I was in awe. But people kept standing up, then sitting down, then standing, then kneeling on a little padded bench. Up...down… kneel…down…up… The preacher wore a long dress and I couldn't understand a word he was saying. Whether it was in Latin or I just couldn't hear, it didn't matter. I was confused from the standing, sitting and kneeling.

Later, we occasionally attended a Baptist Church where a charismatic pastor became loud, angry and red in the face as he shouted hellfire and damnation. I was always afraid his head was going to explode, and my mother always cried near the end of the service. I was never sure if her tears were because she feared the preacher, or because I had done something or for some other reason. I liked the music, though, and grew to cherish some of the old Southern gospel I learned there, even if I didn't hear some of the words correctly.

"Blessed insurance (assurance), Jesus is mine. Oh what a forest (foretaste)of glory be mine (divine)…" I sang at the top of my asthmatic lungs.

I wasn't sure if Jesus was mine. In fact I wasn't even sure who or what Jesus was, in spite of several years of Vacation Bible School at various houses of worship. I was there for the craft projects, Kool-Aid and vanilla wafers.

My occasional prayers at that age were rote and meaningless, and true spirituality eluded me. But Dad was very proud when I sang the words to *Softly and Tenderly* perfectly. It was one of his favorites, and I was thrilled when he harmonized with me right there in the kitchen, playing his acoustic guitar. The reason I knew that particular song so well was because Mom had a recording of a guy called Tennessee Ernie Ford singing it. The song became the first hymn in my piano repertoire, and the old gospel I learned as a child became an avenue to spirituality as an adult.

❧

One time when we were visiting Tennessee, Dad stopped at a road-side storefront that sold ice cream cones. Happily licking our frozen treats, we followed Dad like the Pied Piper, through the gravel parking lot where I noticed the sound of music coming from beside an old wagon. What I found there changed my life.

A small group of acoustic musicians were playing string instruments. A dark-haired woman sang and slapped a huge upright bass for all it was worth. I had never seen anyone playing this instrument before and had never seen a woman do anything except sing. The package shows which came to the high school auditoriums featured the top country performers and their bands but never had I seen a woman as part of a band. Their role always seemed to be more that of eye candy or window dressing as the 'featured girl singer," and not really an integral piece of the music.

Still holding the now forgotten ice cream, I stared. I wanted to do this.

I noticed there was a guy playing a guitar. Watching him nimbly strum the chords reminded me of Dad, who was standing nearby. Finally, my eyes came to rest on a tall, dark young man who was playing the banjo. He reminded me of the character Jethro Bodine from the Beverly Hillbillies on television. In fact, that was where I had heard this kind of music before. I was transfixed. His fingers moved faster than I could comprehend and he was the handsomest boy I had ever seen, in person anyway. He couldn't have been more than 18 or 20 years old - maybe even closer to my age, I thought hopefully. When he turned and stared directly back at me, grinned and winked, I froze.

With ice cream now running down my elbow and mouth agape, I couldn't breathe. This was the first time any male younger than my Grandpa had openly shown any sign of flirtatious interest. He *winked*! At ME! I was rooted to the ground. This was definitely new territory. I *really* liked Tennessee now!

I floated back to the car and so began my lifelong love affair with bluegrass music.

As a child, I managed to stay more or less unaware of the tensions and anxiety present in our household. This changed, however, as I grew older.

As I entered the world of formal education, I began developing a tacit awareness of the emotional chaos and negativity surrounding much of our lives. I remember eventually feeling somehow to blame for what went on at home, responsible for my mother's tears and my father's anger, a role I later assumed with relish, driving them both nearly nuts.

In 1963, we moved into the small, ranch-style house in Janesville, Wis., where Mom and Dad still live – the place I think of as home. This is where most of my memories are, but during the time I lived there I chafed at the bit, especially as I grew older. I felt restless, confined and anxious for the time when I could leave forever.

At home, I awoke mornings to the smell of coffee and, whenever Dad was home, cigarette smoke. Mom had the local radio station on daily, usually playing country music and giving the weather report. Clark and I walked across the street and caught a yellow school bus each day, our breath turning to vapor in the gray light of subzero Wisconsin winters.

School might have been a positive social outlet, but it wasn't. Chubby, with thick glasses and kinky, naturally curly hair, I was different from the other kids. Always in poor health and with many allergies, I was plagued by anxiety and self-doubt by the time I was 9.

I had constant ear infections, so my teeth were discolored from ingesting powerful antibiotics and I often had putrid-smelling cotton stuffed in one or both ears.

I also missed a lot of school because of lung problems. Sometimes it felt like there was a revolving door at the hospital for me, but these visits were made bearable because the nurses made a big fuss over my extra-long eyelashes. Also, I got presents.

But then it was back to school, and the presents were forgotten in the wake of peer ridicule. Having no friends to play with at recess and no one to talk to on the playground underscored a childhood that already felt lonely.

I won several talent contests throughout the years by playing the piano, but it did nothing to increase my shaky confidence or self-esteem, nor did it win me any friends. I slowly withdrew, even while trying hard to fit in. I probably tried too hard. I had nothing in common with kids my age but yearned for just one friend.

I loved it when Willie Ruth Bentley, Mom's best friend from high school, came for the occasional visit or when we visited her family in a neighboring state. My parents usually seemed happy and behaved well when others were present, especially Willie Ruth.

Willie sewed clothes for my cousins and me while we were still infants and made me a baby quilt that I kept until it became thin, tattered shreds of material and no longer useable, some time in my 40s. Even then, I was reluctant to part with this hand-made memento of the unconditional love I felt from this woman.

When I was a preschooler, Willie Ruth even ordered me a fancy birthday cake from a bakery, all decked out like a carousel. In those days, a lop-sided homemade cake with some candles on it was the norm for most working-class families. I was so enchanted with the carousel confection that I remember not wanting anyone to eat it!

Sometimes I felt like Willie Ruth loved me more than my own parents did. Her daughter, Diana, was just a couple of years older than I was. Diana and I talked, laughed and played with Barbie dolls and I had a great friend, if only until it was time for them or us to leave.

Prior to the fourth grade, I wanted to be a teacher. My 30 dolls had the best education an aspiring young instructor could give them. I lined them up in my room on my bed, sometimes grouping them according to age and skill levels. Sleeping Beauty, with her long, blue satin gown, was always my smartest pupil, though I tried to be fair and not show favoritism.

Anytime I could coerce someone into playing school, I was in heaven. I taught my father, my brother, several playmates and even Fluffles, our cat. Eagerly, I eagerly volunteered for summer school and was an avid reader.

In the fourth grade, I had the first of many major ear surgeries, missing weeks of school. My teacher, whom I thought to be at least 120 years old with her ample bosom, pointed yellow teeth, and steely, grayish-yellow hair braided around her head, assured us that everything would be fine. When I got back, however, I was lost. Especially in arithmetic.

One of her favorite exercises called for students to go to the chalkboard to do math problems, but I had no idea what to do. I stood there uncertainly with cotton in my ear, the last child up in front of the room. With chalk in hand, without a clue, distracted and self-conscious, I listened in vain as our formidable instructor attempted to bring me up to speed in front of everyone. I only grew more confused and wished the floor would swallow me.

She got mad, stomped her feet, yelled loudly and became red in the face while the other kids snickered. I wanted to run. She turned her head away and shook with rage at my inept, feeble attempts to solve the problem.

Mortified, I now wanted to die but simply hung my head and stood there for what seemed like hours. She finally came over and forcefully grabbed the chalk from my hand, finishing the assignment for me and breaking the chalk in the process. Thoroughly humiliated, I could then finally sit down. Her disgust weighed heavily upon my small shoulders and I never did well in math after that.

Chapter 2

Adolescent Hell and a garage band

Her name was Joanne and she lived in a meadow by a pond …

- Joanne, Michael Nesmith

Never popular, and with a hearing deficit now, in addition to my other differences, I was beginning to feel like a pariah. I couldn't participate in many of the activities my fellow classmates did, especially if they were of a physical nature. I dreaded gym class, with our hideously unflattering uniforms, where I was always the last to be picked for any team.

I sat on the bleachers during swim class, under doctor's orders not to get my problem ear wet. And of course, I was still totally lost in mathematics.

At a time when peers were all-important, none would give me the time of day. I was a dweeb, a dork and a pathetic loser. No one liked me, not even me.

By seventh grade, I was an angry adolescent. This anger was directed toward my parents, my brother and myself because it had nowhere else to go.

My rebelliousness knew no bounds. Full of stress and inner turmoil, I was a small, female James Dean. Although some would politely suggest that I reminded them more of Bug's Bunny's nemesis, the Tasmanian Devil.

My mirror became my worst enemy as I tried to fix the outer me. I dyed my hair red. Then black. Then I experimented with make-up to the extreme. Then I pulled out all my eyebrows and lashes.

I cut my hair haphazardly during rages and bit my fingernails. Shaking with frustration before school, I became a source of anxiety and tension in the household. I was on the verge of a meltdown most of the time.

Reading was my refuge. I read everything I could get my hands on. If I watched television, I read a book during the commercials. It became a personal challenge to see how fast I could get through *Gone with the Wind*, lusting after Rhett Butler before I even knew what lust was.

I read newspapers, flyers and the TV guide. Sitting at the kitchen table, I ate cereal with the boxes arranged around me like a small fortress and read the ads, the offers and even the nutritional panels on the sides. Probably my preoccupation with the written word was a response to the isolation I felt in my life and the cereal box barrier was indicative of my desire to hide. The only friend I had throughout junior high school was Jo Ann, who much later became my sister-in-law.

Our house was directly across the street from the city limits sign and was a picture of the modest, urban 1960s blue-collar American dream. We had a fairly large front yard and close neighbors.

Jo Ann lived on a working farm far from town with no nearby neighbors.

Because of her rural roots, she, like me, felt different and lonely.

With no brothers or sisters close to her own age, she became my surrogate sister. We visited each other's homes as often as possible, slept over, ate lunch at school together, went downtown and discovered boys and beer, although I never really liked the taste. Of beer, that is.

My visits to her family farm were a comedy of errors, largely because I was allergic to almost everything in her environment, inside and out. She had chores to do, something with which I was totally unfamiliar, so I would wait inside the house, tissues in hand and allergy medication nearby. Upon finishing her duties in the barn and with the livestock, she would come back in, wearing huge galoshes and work clothes, which I found hilarious.

She found me equally entertaining with my swollen, itchy red eyes, wheezing and often sneezing uncontrollably by then. We would both begin laughing so hard we couldn't stop. Trying to squelch our giggles so as not to wake the rest of the household in the night made the situation even more humorous. We laughed ourselves silly, still trying not to make a sound. Sleep came eventually, the result of exhaustion from the almost silent laughter and the security found in the company of a best friend.

My parents accepted her as family, and she stuck up for me at school, which I thought was the noblest thing anyone could do. Kids can be very cruel, and they were.

"You are *sooo* ugly," mumbled Bobby Sillan, between classes.

"Don't sit beside *me*," said another classmate.

Dennis Schirtz sneered at me for a whole year in English class.

Another group of girls made it a point to hold their noses every time they passed me in the hallway. These friendly overtures were common in my world.

When I was fourteen years old, I visited my glamorous cousin Lois Johnson, who was in show business in Nashville, Tenn. Attempting to deal with my unruly, naturally curly hair, she got me a long straight hairpiece that attached with a headband. When I came back to school, I wore it daily, hoping to fool people into thinking it was my own sleek new hairdo.

I felt pretty wearing it and didn't fuss before the mirror for 45 minutes in the morning anymore. I covered up my monstrous mop of frizz and thought no one would know the difference. It didn't improve my popularity, but it did improve my self-esteem somewhat until one night Jo Ann and I went downtown.

In 1969, before the era of astronomical gas prices, anyone who had access to a car cruised round and round the seven-block stretch in downtown Janesville known as the 'circuit.' This was a gathering place for teens and an informal social venue for the area. Revving one's engine at a stoplight, feigning indifference to those on the sidewalk while the Doors or Led Zeppelin loudly blared from your radio was the epitome of cool.

The sound of car horns, engines and radios filled the street on this balmy evening. Jo Ann and I were walking near a bridge on the main drag when we were approached by a group of girls we recognized from school. I thought of them as the "tough" girls and tread lightly. We acknowledged one another in passing.

Suddenly, one of them turned and pushed me down on the sidewalk, tearing off my faux hair. Jo Ann was shocked and indignant, and we were both caught by surprise. I was unhurt, but my pride was devastated and I went home swearing never to return to junior high. I had a full-blown case of scolionophobia, the scientific term for fear of school.

My sympathetic but frustrated parents knew I would rather have faced a firing squad than to go back to school. Nothing could change my mind. That incident, on top of an already fragile ego and almost no confidence, made me not want to leave my room, and for a time, I considered living under the bed.

My parents, the teachers and principal conferred, I was sent for counseling, and it was decided I could do schoolwork assignments at home.

During much of this period of my life, I was miserable. The tiny thread of hope within me fed on Jo Ann's friendship as well as the sometimes misguided but well-intentioned love of my family. The world of books kept me from having to deal with the everyday realities that brought me down and I dreamed of the soft, blue-gray mountains of Tennessee. My long-term plan was to escape there.

Soon, I discovered music in a bigger way, visiting the nearby practice shack of a local rock band whenever possible. The power that these long-haired musicians exerted collectively through their instruments was awesome and greater than anything I had experienced before.

I spent hours in the psychedelic day glow world of Cream, Black Sabbath, and the assorted cornucopia of music of the late '60s and early '70s, which gave me an outlet, a legitimate avenue and voice for my rebellion. It provided comfort and fueled dreams that would later see me through other storms in life. My record player became my most valuable possession.

Luckily, there was only a short time left until school ended after the downtown incident, so I did a few assignments from my bedroom refuge and was promoted to high school.

George S. Parker High School seemed huge. We were all scheduled into different classes, and there were many new faces that hadn't declared themselves my enemy or known how stupid I was in the fourth grade.

With a little more anonymity, I felt somewhat better about formal education, but the damage had been done. I genuinely tried to do well but discovered I was easily bored. After a year or so of this, I dropped out and convinced my parents that I would do better living with my aunt and graduating from my mother's alma mater in my beloved Tennessee. Escape at last!

Although my mother had been a "Yankee" and called Wisconsin home, her family had traveled a great deal due to my grandfather's profession as a sheet metal worker. He worked on defense contracts, and they spent time in Oklahoma, Illinois and eventually, East Tennessee, where they stayed long enough for Mother to graduate from high school and meet my dad. The rest, as they say, is history.

Dad took me to his sister - my tiny, sweet Aunt Lucille - in Powell, Tenn., and I began high school anew there. Eager for a fresh start, I was thrilled at this chance; however, after about six weeks, I experienced ongoing flu-like symptoms. Although I didn't want to be any trouble or cause problems, things seemed to get worse.

A doctor gave me green pills and diagnosed me as being homesick. I already knew I missed my family, but I didn't know that being homesick could actually make you feel queasy and weak. With no improvement, I was taken to two more doctors, one of whom hospitalized me for observation.

That night I asked a nurse for some crackers or something to eat.

"Maybe we can find something, let me check and see if you're allowed to have anything. I'll be right back," she said in an East Tennessee twang.

"Uhh....maybe something to drink too....?" I hollered toward the doorway where she had just been standing.

Upon her return, she informed me I was to have exploratory surgery in the morning. No crackers for me.

The next thing I heard upon waking was that my parents were there to visit me. My arms felt wooden and my legs like lead. I had no idea what was wrong. My eyes would hardly stay open, and I was so groggy I could barely think, but teenage vanity ever present, I was putting on makeup when they came in.

Mom, Dad and Clark all entered my room looking as if they'd been crying. I had no idea why they were there or how they could have gotten from Wisconsin to Tennessee so quickly. Under sedation, 10 hours had become 10 minutes.

Apparently, when my father called the hospital to find out how the surgery went, he was advised to get there as soon as possible. My condition was critical. The pathologist's report said that my appendix had been leaking for 10 to 12 days and I was consumed with peritonitis.

Remembering that night, I realized I was sick, but didn't know just how serious it was until later. I was glad to see my family and Dad stayed with me all night in the hospital room. I drifted in and out of sleep and pain. Abdominal surgery hurt a lot worse than ear surgery.

Very late, when all was quiet, dark and still, I felt myself slowly rise from the bed and move up toward the ceiling, as if I were floating. But I could see my body still lying in the bed below. I knew that was me lying there with an IV in my arm, but another part of me was light as air, somehow transcending time, matter and gravity.

"How odd," I thought to myself, strangely detached. "I know this is not a dream...." Although this was a puzzling new experience, I was not alarmed.

From up near the ceiling, where it seemed that I was now hovering, I saw Dad sitting on the foot of the bed, facing the wall, his head in his hands. I thought he was crying but wasn't sure. Knowing he was concerned about me, I wanted to comfort him but couldn't. Looking out the window of my fourth floor room, I saw the river below and the city lights of Knoxville, Tenn. I noticed a vent of some kind in the ceiling nearby, then looked back down to the hospital bed where my body was still lying peacefully in the sterile sheets.

It was as if I were an observer of a surreal scene from someone else's life. At the same time, there was a sense of tranquility that I had never known and a momentary lightness of being that filled me with love and compassion. I felt happy and completely free.

In just a few moments, inexplicably, I was back in my bed and my body once again. Somehow, there was no confusion. I felt calm and much of the anger and anxiety of my young life seemed to be gone as well as any pain during those few moments when I had floated high above the room.

There were no tunnels or bright, white lights as I've heard described in near-death experiences. If I were hallucinating, it was rather mundane and short-lived. I have no explanations but I remembered that experience throughout the years as vividly as if it were yesterday.

Four days later, on my 17th birthday, I was pronounced out of danger and served birthday cake, my first real food since the surgery.

Mom, Dad and Clark had to fly back to Wisconsin. I stayed in the hospital for almost a month.

Music was now my panacea and salvation, and I had my portable record player at my bedside. Often, I visited the hospital chapel alone, especially late in the evening, where I played the organ and piano and sometimes sang.

"Blessed insurance, Jesus is mine...Oh what a forest..." Just kidding. By now, I knew the right words.

Other times, I visited an area on another floor that looked out to my precious friendly mountains.

I had a phone by my bed, occasional visitors and regular wheelchair races with orderlies, but there was no getting around the fact that I was now really homesick. Even my favorite rock and rollers, the Rolling Stones and Rod Stewart, couldn't ease the ache I felt in my heart or the longing for my immediate family. Maybe home was wherever family was.

I mended slowly. When well enough to leave, I left Aunt Lucille's and headed back to Janesville.

Dad always wanted the best of everything for us. One year, Santa, who silently visited us each Christmas Eve until we were well into adulthood, brought me a big double-keyboard console Lowrey organ, like a church organ. It didn't matter that I only wanted a small, portable, combo organ to play in a band, my career of choice. That same year, my brother Clark, who wanted a mini-bike, got the smallest trail motorcycle manufactured by Honda.

Before I ever left for Tennessee, Clark and I began making music, he on his electric guitar and I on my hands and knees playing bass on the foot pedals of the Lowrey, or occasionally up on the keyboard, toes stretching toward the bass pedals.

Iron Butterfly's *Inna-gadda-da-vida* or a version of *Whiter Shade of Pale*, both classics from the era, graced our living room regularly as I imagined myself at a Hammond B-3, performing for thousands of people holding lit cigarette lighters high in homage.

While I was in Tennessee, Clark and Gary, a buddy from the neighborhood, began having band practice. Gary didn't quite have a drum set yet, but he had drumsticks and happily played my parents' old metal dehumidifier in the basement for hours, jamming with Clark. Mom and Dad probably had the only dehumidifier in town pockmarked with indentations from the percussion section.

Also while I was gone, a new kid had moved in down the block who fancied himself a bass guitar player and singer. They had a *real band* now – and they had been practicing in Mom and Dad's garage. I was jealous and wanted in on the action.

I also had a strange, unidentifiable gut feeling about the new kid. The instant I heard about him over the phone, while still at my Aunt Lucille's, I knew through some weird psychic connection that he would play a big role in my future.

I knew his name before my mother spoke it, visualized his face, which I had never seen before, and instinctively knew my destiny was at hand.

A garage band and my first real love awaited me.

Chapter 3

Stardom awaits

I'm gonna live forever, I'm gonna learn how to fly
I feel it coming together, People will see me and cry
I'm gonna make it to heaven, Light up the sky like a flame
I'm gonna live forever, Baby remember my name

- Fame, Irene Cara

Lois, my Nashville-based cousin, was my idol. She had been in the country music business since childhood, performing on the *Cas Walker Show* and the *Mid-Day Merry-Go-Round* over the airwaves out of Knoxville, Tenn. She later worked with bluegrass legend Jimmy Martin, country icon Ernest Tubb, was friends with Ralph Emery and recorded with Hank Williams Jr.

She had worked with almost everyone who was anyone in the country music industry from that era and had several hits of her own. When I was very young, I recall her taking me backstage somewhere. As I peered out from behind the curtains at the huge audience, even then I thought, "*This* is for me!"

Loving all kinds of music ever since I could remember, I relaxed listening to Dad sing lullabies or pick the guitar Chet Atkins style. His version of *Wildwood Flower* was reminiscent of the early Carter Family sound and his songs were from what we now call roots music of southern Appalachia. He didn't attend church much but his gospel songs were from the heart and I learned the basics at his knee.

My mother's rollicking version of "The Old Grey Mare" was entertaining if not professional. A particularly memorable treat was Mom, with mischief in her eye, grinning and dancing in the kitchen. Early or old school soul music with it's thumping rhythm and anything by Wilson Pickett sent her into spasms of gyrating rhythm, much to the amusement of the rest of the family and anyone else who happened to be around.

She firmly declared, and still maintains, that she wants these songs played at her funeral someday.

Throughout the angst and uncertainty of my teen years, I always found solace in music. It was my drug of choice, my companion and my dream. Even today, like many other people, listening to or playing music has the power to change my mood and influence my actions.

When I returned home to Wisconsin, I started down the stairs to the basement where the fledgling band was practicing and met Dave, a skinny, pimply kid with dirty blond hair and a slight attitude. His was the face that had flashed before me while talking to Mom on the phone when I was still at Aunt Lucille's and at age 17, I was smitten.

I joined the band, and we were all off on the adventure of a lifetime.

By now I had traded the Lowrey organ for a more portable Farfisa keyboard. Thinking we were well on our way to stardom, we knew six songs when a friend asked us to play in the gymnasium of the Wisconsin School for the Visually Handicapped.

Honored and excited, we hurried to learn a few more songs for our public debut. Playing for a live audience was definitely more fun and exciting than playing in my parents' garage or basement. Then my friend Patti called and told us her employer needed a band for the next week. She asked if we wanted to audition.

The Evergreen, a combination bar and restaurant in Janesville, Wis., might not have been the big time, but it may as well have been to us. *Of course* we wanted to audition! We probably would have paid someone to listen to us, but even the remote possibility of making money legitimized and validated our efforts. Just the opportunity to audition meant we were now showbiz professionals!

Thrilled beyond measure when we actually got the job, we thought of this as our big break.

Most of us were not old enough to drive, let alone be in bars and nightclubs. We would be required to have somebody's parent or guardian accompany us each evening. Dave's mom and dad were as thrilled as we were and immediately volunteered to be our chaperones. The only stumbling block was that our Dad was against the whole idea from the beginning. Although not a prude, overtly religious or judgmental person, he was not a drinker and wasn't comfortable with his kids being in bars.

We couldn't believe that he would stand in the way of our dreams or block our path to stardom. The other parents had no such qualms, we were overwhelmed with excitement and soon he relented, to our relief.

The Evergreen smelled of stale beer and cigarette smoke and was so dimly lit that the neon lights of the jukebox were all that could be seen upon first entering. We nervously set up our equipment early and tried to contain our excitement as we began the first set.

"...Blue, blue... blue suede shoes..." sang Dave. Elvis was a surefire crowd-pleaser.

Clark, being very shy, wouldn't turn around and face the audience. He played to his amplifier all night. Gary said his knees were knocking so loudly he was afraid they would drown out his new drum set. I turned my head slightly to look out the window behind the stage and saw a fight in progress in the parking lot. Still playing my keyboard, I kept an eye on the action and silently rooted for the chubby guy who had been nice to me when we came in.

"...so get offa my blue suede shoes..." sang Dave for the second time that night.

We still didn't know very many songs and someone had drawn a knife out in the parking lot. A couple of people got out on the dance floor. Several others approached us with requests, which we promised to learn.

I was as nervous as Clark and Gary, but Dave, my hero, appeared to be a pillar of courage and the picture of confidence. We all drew strength from him. This was our star, our front man extraordinaire, and the one elected to do all the talking. He admitted later that he was so scared he thought he was going to be sick.

It looked like another fight might be brewing in the parking lot but most of the patrons were content to nurse their drinks quietly. We took it all in stride and tried to act sophisticated beyond our years, but were secretly thrilled and just kept playing the few songs we knew well and a few we didn't know quite as well.

"….You can do anything but don't step on my blue suede shoes…." Dave sang once again.

The owner told us we were doing a good job and paid us in cash toward the end of the evening.

Making it through the first weekend, the little team of future superstars were both exhilarated and exhausted. We were a big hit, probably because we were such a novelty, as young as we were.

To us, it was all part of a wild evening that felt like the beginning of something big!

For the next couple of years, our band, Tumbleweed Rock, was one of the most popular, busiest groups in Southern Wisconsin, and of course, we eventually learned more songs. Not a week went by that we weren't booked somewhere and our success surprised even us. We even did a live, remote radio broadcast in March of 1972.

I became very comfortable with crowds and the music was second nature to me. It came easily, and I loved the high I got from a good night.

When all of us were in the groove, familiar tunes took on new dynamics. The crowd was with us, traveling wherever the music led and we were at the epicenter. It was a very powerful and heady feeling. Gary, Clark, Dave and I were united through unique experiences, and our star burned brightly.

Eventually Dad and Mom came to see our show. Although they remained teetotalers, they danced a little at the various clubs and venues where we performed, including a retirement party at the company for which my dad worked. We even got Dad up on stage to pick a little guitar, but you could tell he wasn't comfortable. I eventually came to feel that both of our parents were very proud of their children for the first time.

I soon discovered that having any sort of talent in the arts was a passport to acceptance in some circles, a fact that remains true at every level of our society even today. The same can be said of sports figures.

There is a special place in our culture for those with natural gifts and the inclination, initiative and ability to develop them. In fact, sometimes we make special allowances for these folks that may not be in their best interest. More about that later.

Now beginning to have the self-esteem and capability to think creatively and independently, I had established an identity as a performer and nonconformist. Painting one wall of my bedroom black, I hung a huge silk screen print of Jimi Hendrix, mounted a black light and reveled in being different. Janis Joplin was my new hero.

If Dad was in a bad mood or Mom was crying, I just shut them out. I could shut out the whole world for hours at a time, high on the music that played on my record player or with my nose still in a book.

Dave, now more or less my boyfriend, encouraged me not to care about what others thought and to do my own thing. He made me feel worthwhile and special and instilled in me a whole new attitude. Very cool with his custom-sewn, tight bell-bottom blue jeans and cowboy boots, he had star power written all over him at age 15.

His talent was awesome, but my vision was colored by how deeply I had already fallen for him. We were friends, band mates, neighbors, schoolmates and fellow members of the "revolution." Our attitudes had an edge that cut when directed at each other - and it often was. As the relationship progressed, we would be together, then break up, then get back together, then try to be friends, then fight, then date others, then get back together again.

I spent innumerable hours at his house and he at mine. In fact, the entire neighborhood now congregated in our cement block basement, where we held band practice regularly. Mom and Dad didn't seem to mind. I guess they knew where we were, at least. Dad even acted as an informal lay counselor of sorts for some of our friends during this period. This included Dave one night when he drunkenly appeared, sitting in the middle of our driveway in need of sympathy and advice, which Dad patiently dispensed.

If you wanted to find someone from the neighborhood, chances are, they were in our basement. Decorated with Yellow Submarine stickers, Beatles posters, colored light bulbs and a wooden double door leading outside from the basement that was autographed by all who entered, there was surprisingly little illicit activity. Most of the kids respected our parents and did their underage drinking off the premises although bottles were often stashed nearby.

I got to know Dave's family and other families in the neighborhood as well as my own.

One night, soon after I got my driver's license, Dave's sister Linda and I were speeding back from a neighboring town trying to beat our midnight curfew. I was madly driving my parents' old white station wagon on a straight, two-lane country road when a voice inside my head said, "slow down."

Immediately I lifted my foot off the gas completely, the speedometer fell back to 60 mph and I felt a jerk just as we hit loose gravel on the deserted pavement. Skidding, the car lurched crazily, completely out of control, toward the darkness at the edge of the road. The steering wheel spun violently, the headlights sliced into the black night sky at a crazy angle and I held my breath. It happened so fast that we didn't have time to react. The car rolled end over end, coming to rest, lights still on, in what appeared to be a field. The windows were shattered and the back seat was now in the middle of the car. After a moment of stunned silence, I asked Linda if she was all right.

"I...I guess so," she replied, wide-eyed.

Somewhat in shock at still being alive, we ended up at the hospital where I think Linda may have had a slight scratch on her hand. I was completely unhurt, but shaken. Later, we found that the car's right rear tire had blown just as we hit the loose gravel. Skidding out of control, we thudded to a sudden stop about 10 feet from a huge open rock quarry pit. I hadn't even known it was there.

It could have been much, much worse. I solemnly swore to myself that I would drive more carefully in the future and my lead foot was somewhat tempered for the time being.

Three houses down from where we lived was a roller skating rink. Nights were often spent gravitating between their parking lot and our basement or downtown on the Circuit where I once stuffed 14 people into my parents Chevrolet Corvair just to see how many we could fit inside. Ralph Nader would have had a coronary! With people laying in the back window, arranged horizontally across the tops of the bucket seats and appendages hanging out the other windows, it was a traveling party!

The party lasted about five minutes, becoming uncomfortable for all involved, but it was indicative of our idea of fun at the time.

The members of the band all had more money than we knew what to do with, easy cash money. We played country-western music, as it was called at the time, the more upbeat popular music of the day, and oldies. We played all kinds of tunes including novelties like the *Bunny-Hop* and popular ad jingles. Everything was geared toward the enjoyment of the crowd. And for the most part, there were large crowds.

Dave developed into a talented lead vocalist and once in a while, one of us would harmonize. Clark's guitar riffs were sharp, imaginative and original. Gary became a rock-solid drummer and band manager of sorts. He directed the technical side of the operation, packing, setting up and making transportation arrangements while I kept track of bookings and money.

We had publicity pictures taken out in the field behind the house and at the neighbor's old barn up the road. I wore hot pants, a playful term for tight shorts, and we all tried to act tough and mature, especially while in the clubs.

We stuck together, going home to Dave's house or out to eat at 2 a.m. to talk about the night and wind down. It was our way of processing the evening. My mother clipped and saved anything that appeared in print about us.

This was our initiation into adulthood, our own rite of passage, our progression into maturity and we were honored to be part of the world of music. The band gave me a whole new outlook on life, and my deepening relationship with Dave offered self-worth along with a new determination to be all that I could be and expand my horizons.

Going back to high school, I was allowed to take a couple of college classes at the local University of Wisconsin campus, using them for high school credit.

College was very cool. Smoking was allowed, they had "beer night" and even though I didn't partake of either, I appreciated those adult activities in an educational institution. This was a far cry from the classrooms of my past. Instructors put their feet up on tables, and sometimes we went outside for classes. I liked the feeling of freedom.

By virtue of local "stardom," I now had new prestige in high school, where I still attended classes as well.. Not quite one of the popular crowd, I was more aligned with the creative renegade types that you might find in the theater crowd and, indeed, I did find the theater. Or, rather, the theater found me.

Dave was involved in theater classes and had done very well as an actor in school productions. I saw the camaraderie backstage and was jealous of the closeness of cast members, not to mention the female cast members who threw themselves at my talented on-again-off-again boyfriend. I thought an acting class in college would be a piece-of-cake and an easy A, and that was where the theater bug first bit.

My very first role was the leading lady in Sheridan's School for Scandal at the University of Wisconsin, Rock County. The director became a friend, mentor and inspiration. Later on, with different instructors, I would have even greater opportunities in writing and directing, as well as performing on campus. I was no Ethel Barrymore, but I had found a creative home.

Maybe I still wasn't entirely happy with my life or myself, but onstage I could be somebody else for a short time and escape into another world.

Being an actress allowed me access to doors previously closed and gave me an excuse to try on other personalities and try out new experiences, all without risk. And like most performers, I thrived on the applause. That became the seal of approval that had been lacking from much of my childhood and the catalyst for building a confidence I'd never had.

Eventually, I got my high school diploma. It was late, but better late than never. Probably the principal just got tired of seeing me around and did me a favor. I never got to wear a prom dress or mortarboard and tassel but I made up for it later.

Chapter 4

Marilyn Monroe and motherhood

Somebody told me when I got to Nashville
Son you finally got it made
Old Hank made it here, we're all sure that you will
But I don't think Hank done it this way
I don't think Hank done it this way

- Are you Sure Hank Done it this Way, Waylon Jennings

I had followed Dave's lead becoming involved in theater and had now performed leading roles in high school and in college. I had written, directed and produced a children's musical in December of 1977 and been initiated into a drama organization.

Dave had won an award in high school for a performance, but when I won one the next year and he didn't, he wouldn't speak to me for a week. He began to occasionally have fits of jealousy and rage, but still made me feel loved and wanted.

We were close confidantes and more or less consistent lovers but it was still a tempestuous relationship.

We had both felt ourselves outcasts and this united us. Neither of us came from idyllic home lives, which became a bond as well.

Dave had experimented with illegal substances but alcohol was the most easily accessible and the drug of choice for most of our peers. By the time he was 15 or 16, he was already a heavy drinker, not unusual for that time and place. Gary was following suit and Clark, the youngest, was trying hard to keep up.

I didn't know what normal was as far as alcohol consumption. Almost everyone we knew drank. It was a way of life.

I had no idea what "normal" was for a home life either. The ups and downs with my parents over the years translated into a roller coaster relationship pattern that I thought was love. And maybe it was, but maybe it was more of a codependency, something I'd never heard of in the early '70's.

I never quite recovered from my hospital stay in East Tennessee and after extensive testing, it was discovered that I had Crohn's disease, a chronic inflammatory intestinal illness for which there was no known cure. No one knew what caused it and there could be many complications leading to colostomy bags and even death.

Some people suffering from this disease are visibly weakened, pale and have the ravaged appearance of one battling major illness. Some lose too much weight whereas others may have a bloated appearance from side effects of medications. I only wished I could suffer the weight loss that sometimes accompanies a flare up. I leaned toward the pleasingly plump end of the scale. But like all youth, I was sure I would live forever and was oblivious to the severity of my illness.

The various medications prescribed didn't seem to work and surgery was required, removing two feet of my intestine at the University of Wisconsin Hospital in Madison at age 18.

Abdominal surgery was once again agonizing, but the whole procedure was worth it when my family brought along my beloved Dave to visit me at the hospital. I was also released on a weekend pass to play a gig. I had never missed one. It was one for all and all for one, and the show must go on. The surgery was apparently successful because I had no problems for more than 17 years afterward.

Soon, the stage had become my identity. It defined who I was, whether through music or theater. I was determined to become a superstar and aligned myself closely with images of Marilyn Monroe, thinking at times that perhaps I channeled her, another term I'd never heard in the mid-'70s.

Thinking no one understood Marilyn better than I did, I delved into her life, pouring over books, movies, articles and anything I could find about her. I merged our personalities into one and "became" Marilyn to the public, but without her apparent dependence on narcotics. My narcotic was Dave.

For the most part, we were inseparable. Even when his family moved to Rockford, Ill., about 30 miles away, we were still together as much as possible. The bond between us became the one thing that we could each count on. I felt lost without him, and most of the time I thought he felt that way about me. We spent hours on the phone, talking about everything and nothing, laughing softly into the night.

During our time together, he wrote me poems and songs. I was Dale Evans to his Roy Rogers, Ginger Rogers to his Fred Astaire, Cher to his Sonny.

When you are with someone all the time and you see them regularly, you may not notice that they have gained or lost weight, developed wrinkles or their hair has turned gray. It's when you don't see someone in a while, like at class reunions, that you particularly notice these things.

In this way, I didn't notice what Dave or our relationship was becoming.

No one in my immediate family was a drinker. I knew Dave's parents were heavy drinkers, but I adored them. They always seemed to have so much fun when they went out with the band. And they seemed so accepting of me. But there was a dark side, triggered by substance abuse, that I would later see in Dave.

The young man I knew and loved was literate, articulate and intelligent. He was fun loving, witty and uninhibited. Once, when our family took him with us to Tennessee, he gleefully jumped into the motel pool at midnight fully clothed.

He and Richard, our neighbor, would stay up until dawn improvising Monty Python-esque comedy scripts for imaginary radio shows. They provided ongoing entertainment for each other and anyone else around. Dave was charming, multi-talented, unique and very appealing to women of all ages.

I didn't notice his increasing dependency on controlled substances over the years. I probably wouldn't have recognized the signs of alcoholism. I knew nothing about addictions.

When he went into a jealous rage, I actually found it slightly reassuring. When he threw his guitar across a parking lot after a performance, I thought it was just a bad night. When he rolled a joint, I paid no attention. I stayed. I loved him very much and thought if you truly loved someone, you stayed through anything. After all, my parents had stayed together through everything.

As they say, all good things must come to an end and eventually, the band broke up. It was fun while it lasted; we had a good run and all remained friends but it was time to go our separate ways.

We were tired and each torn in different directions. Clark wanted to play hard core heavy-metal rock and roll, Dave wanted to play pure country music, Gary just needed some time off and I didn't know what I wanted.

I took other jobs and played with other bands. I worked in manufacturing and hospitality, became a weekend demonstrator/spokesperson for food products and more. I traveled some and still harbored dreams of being an actress. But I was still in love with Dave and getting a bit frustrated, wondering where this part-time relationship was leading. I also wanted new challenges.

Finally, Dave and I seemed to be at a crossroads or perhaps a stalemate. I knew I was tired of his crazy lifestyle. Now living with his brother in a dingy downtown apartment, they partied nightly and didn't seem to take anything seriously. Lois, my talented cousin, was performing near Milwaukee, and in the spring of 1978 I decided to go back to Nashville with her on the tour bus.

Many musicians from remote areas harbored vague dreams of Nashville - Music City, USA - where people go to be discovered. Unless, of course you are an actress, in which case you head for Hollywood. I didn't have a ride to Hollywood.

Tinseltown may have been the home of broken dreams, but Nashville was home to melancholy melodies from the pages of life, and, like Hollywood, it was also the land of immortal success.

Hank William's lonely shadow dogged the footsteps of the hopeful in a town then adorned with star-spangled suits, big hair on men as well as women and the Grand Ole Opry, where all gathered to worship the art form that was country music.

Music Row was the heart of the gold rush and I thought I was, at last, heading to someplace I really felt I belonged. Maybe my earlier vision of myself as Marilyn Monroe was slightly off. Maybe I should have channeled Patsy Cline instead.

Once in Nashville, however, I found that not all was glamour and stage lights. One didn't necessarily run into Johnny Cash on the sidewalk and the country music stars did not all regularly have tea or anything else with one another. Most shows occurred out on the road and when a show was over, it was back to the bus and on to the next town and the next audience. And after a while, they all begin to look the same.

I discovered that traveling by bus, even a decked-out Silver Eagle, is somewhat tedious and that recording music in the studio is very repetitive - not at all exciting, when you get right down to it.

Doors did not magically open, nor were country music stars beating a path to my door begging for my services on the keyboard. Although the music felt warm, familiar and intimate, the city itself felt cold, competitive and distant. I didn't have a car or know anyone except Lois, and it soon felt like the music business wasn't happening for me in Nashville. Slightly disappointed and bored, I spied an ad for auditions at Chaffin's Barn, a local dinner theater. They were casting actors and actresses for an upcoming show. Hmmm…Should I go back to the theater – in Nashville?

Convincing Lois to take me to the audition, I scored my first paid acting gig. Here I was in Nashville geared up for the music business and I was now an actress again. I decided to take that shot at the spotlight and did well according to all reports.

While playing in the band, I had developed an intuitive knack for reading an audience and felt more at home onstage than off most of the time. This was put to good use in any live performance situation. If a performer is comfortable and enjoying him or herself, chances are, the audience will too.

I lived upstairs at the theater with the other actors and spent days with my buddies Rick and Scotty, whom I'd met during rehearsals. We visited Rick's stately, turn-of-the-century family home on a Civil War battlefield and I had a crush on Scotty, the theater owner's son.

Sometimes other cast members and I went into town for lunch or shopping in the old van provided by the theater company. I had friends now and wasn't a bit homesick. I occasionally missed Dave, but felt like I might be outgrowing him, or beating him at his own game in a way, because I was now a paid, professional actress in Nashville, no less.

I was going somewhere, I smugly thought. He was still playing in sleazy bars in the Midwest, going nowhere.

Feeling I was truly well on my way to stardom, or at least leading the life of a struggling artist, I was full of adventure, hope and who knew what else.

Thoroughly enjoying my time at Chaffin's Barn, we waited on tables and sang *Happy Birthday* to patrons before going upstairs to get ready for the evening's performance.

In *Time Out For Ginger,* I played the supporting role of a spoiled, star-struck 14-year old, who at one point appears onstage in a full-length, Victorian-era, wide hoop skirt, blouse and bonnet.

The stage was set in the middle of the large, open room and had wide steps leading to it from all four corners, where actors entered and exited.

Self-conscious, I often took off my hideously thick glasses while playing in the band, all too aware that they weren't exactly glamorous. This didn't matter while playing in a band since I rarely moved from behind my keyboard.

For this particular production at the theater, I would sometimes remove my spectacles just before I went down the stairs toward the stage; thus, for my entrances, exits and while saying my lines, I couldn't see much beyond my nose.

One of the biggest laughs during the run of the show occurred one evening when I tripped on my long skirt while leaving the stage on the steps I couldn't see.

I took a nosedive, the hoop skirt went straight up and I couldn't regain my footing without it flopping one way or the other. I squirmed and wriggled like a fish out of water. "How in the world did women ever manage these things?" I thought as I distractedly fussed with the hoop, trying to right myself.

I twisted and pulled and sat flat-butted on the floor with the hoop raised up in front of me like an air bag in an automobile.

By this time the audience, as well as the other actors, were focused with amused expressions, on me, the dying fish, who was by then completely out of character.

Everyone was finally treated to a full view of my rear end in period pantaloons, as I pushed the front of the hoop down and raised the back like a giant halo around my head. No longer even making an attempt at dignity or grace and still holding onto my halo, I did a three-legged crawl toward stage left. Fortunately, nothing was hurt but my pride and the new laughs I inadvertently generated more than made up for that.

And so began my tentative venture into physical comedy.

After a one-month run in Nashville, the show was scheduled to move to West Virginia, where there was another dinner theater, then possibly on to Florida.

It was exciting and I was looking forward to the future but the first week in West Virginia I was feeling bloated and not quite fitting into my costumes. I also had several spells where I felt very faint and was, at one point, gripped by profound and intense nausea while walking down the hallway. I barely made it to the bathroom in time and couldn't imagine what could be wrong. I was tired all the time and felt disconnected somehow. My fellow cast members, justifiably concerned, took me to a Charleston doctor.

Sitting on the exam table, I was informed that I was pregnant.

"What do you want to do with it?" asked the female physician.

"*Do* with it?" I asked, in shock and not comprehending.

Told earlier that I might have trouble conceiving due to scarring in my fallopian tubes, I wasn't consistent about using birth control. Dave and I must have said goodbye a little too passionately before I left Wisconsin. I hadn't given the subject enough thought to realize there were options for unplanned pregnancies.

As I numbly sat there on the exam table during those few moments, I remembered a dream I'd had while living at the theater in Nashville of an adorable, light-haired little boy, angelic and beautiful, that I now knew was to be my son. I stared at the floor for a few minutes, taking deep breaths and made several attempts to connect with reality before I quietly said,

"I…I'm g-going to have him, of course…and raise him…and love him"

Chapter 5

Domestic bliss, leaving the trailer park

People smile and tell me I'm the lucky one
And we've just begun, I think I'm gonna have a son

- Danny's Song, Anne Murray

NOT having this child never entered my mind.

I was so sure he was a little boy that I bought baby items in various shades of blue from day one. However, I was confused and uncertain about our future.

Motherhood had never been part of my plan. In fact, I didn't really have a plan other than to pursue show business as far as it would take me. I was primed for the wanderlust and gypsy lifestyle of music and the theater.

My own mother had never overtly encouraged motherhood. She wanted a career for me, something of which she had felt deprived in her day. When Clark and I were old enough to stay alone, she had begun working at a day-old bread store about a mile from our home. I knew she wanted more out of life for me.

When I called to tell my parents the news, Mom refused to speak to me for several weeks. Dad was upset but sympathetic and eventually called back. When I called Dave with the news, he yelled and cursed and also wouldn't speak to me.

In the meantime, I thought about the generous offer of a gay cast member to get married. In the end, I decided my parents, even though I was estranged from them at the moment, wouldn't appreciate a son-in-law who was prettier and more feminine than I was, although he was the sweetest, kindest person I had ever met.

Instead, I got out of my contract as soon as I could. With no money and feeling unwelcome everywhere, I took a bus to the Florence Crittenton Home for Unwed Mothers in Wheeling, W.Va.

They provided a roof over my head and food for my growing belly. At age 22, I was one of the oldest there and didn't know anything about babies. There weren't any in my family and I had almost never baby-sat.

The heavy atmosphere at the home was stifling. I watched these young women, some still almost children themselves, as they laughed, cried, worked, fought and talked together. However, there seemed to be no real kinship and certainly no sense of family or intimacy. It was as if they were simply going through the motions of living. They all knew they were there only temporarily and made no effort to establish real relationships with one another.

Perhaps family and communities had ostracized some for their condition. I assumed that a few, like me, had no real home, at least at the moment.

Several were angry and acted out violently in spite of being in the late stages of pregnancy. Quiet evenings at the home were certainly not what many of them had in mind. We went to doctor appointments in a van, did chores and I kept to myself as much as possible. I was just glad to have a place to live.

Dave was at least speaking to me again and sometimes I would call him collect at night from the kitchen phone. I even called Mom and Dad once or twice, too. Dad now talked to me regularly and finally Mom did, as well.

Dave was still in as much shock as I was originally concerning parenthood. But disbelief subsides faster when you can feel life inside you, and it becomes more real with each gained ounce.

The kindhearted people at the home bought me maternity clothes, which I needed, even though I was not all that far along. I had medical care, but I was sick at heart, desperately missing my family and Dave.

Knowing I was carrying a little bit of him in my womb made me miss him all the more.

I accepted complete and total responsibility for this child after my mother suggested abortion and I declined. I didn't know how I would manage or what I was going to do. I just felt that this child was meant to be, and the prospect of being a mother overshadowed all my previous dreams. Raising him now seemed the ultimate priority, even if I apparently was going to have to do it alone and with no money.

Lonely and confused, I called Dave again. Sober this time for a change, his voice had the soft, loving quality that I had come to know so well. He was still my best friend.

I was a little afraid of giving birth, of the girls at the home and of the future, and he could hear it in my voice.

"Why don't you come on home...?" He asked.

"I...I thought you didn't want me," I whimpered through tears in the deserted kitchen.

"I do love you. Come on back, and... we'll get married," he said.

"You mean it...really...?" I asked, through what were becoming tears of joy.

"Yes. I miss you."

In my present state, it seemed like that was the answer, the right thing to do. This would solve all my problems, I thought.

"I love you," he repeated gently.

"I love you, too," I said. "I'll be home soon."

It was a long bus ride back to Wisconsin for a Labor Day ceremony on the front lawn of my parents' house. I always thought the holiday appropriate since I would be going into labor within several months.

I approached the role of bride from an almost dreamlike state - somehow it didn't feel real, even as it was happening. It felt like when I "married" Mike Monday as a child.

I walked out the kitchen door and down the steps with my dad and my little bouquet. The relatives were all there in chairs, on the same front yard where I had practiced Evel Knieval-type jumps on a homemade ramp with Clark's little motorcycle in the not-so-distant past.

I wore a long white gown, bulging somewhat at the midriff, and Jo Ann was my maid of honor. It was a beautiful, sunny day, and we had planned a reception for that evening at a local nightclub.

Our friend Duane had set up his keyboard near the front porch, where the clergy waited. And waited. And waited.

Dave finally showed up with his arm in a sling, alcohol on his breath and a black eye, in a car with no muffler. He certainly knew how to make an entrance.

Apparently, he and his brother, Russell, who was his best man, had gotten into a fist fight the night before. But at least he showed up.

And when I became a mother in 1978 at age 23, my own mother became "Super-Grammy" to little Brian Jesse, doting over her first grandchild.

Labor was not as hard as I thought it would be, although forceps were required. Brian seemed to smile up at Dave as he held him in the hospital room. We were instantly in love with this sweet bundle of joy and I knew I had made the right choice in having him.

I nursed him for six months, relishing every bit of being a mother and homemaker except I wasn't very good at it. Life had never prepared me for this and my domestic skills were somewhat lacking. In this pre-microwave age, I thought I was a culinary genius by heating a prepackaged frozen entrée and making toast in a toaster, although I did keep a fairly clean house.

Life as a young couple with a baby was hard. My father helped us get a mobile home but money was always scarce. Dave was playing in a band, trying to work at a day job, and also still drinking heavily. He often stayed out later than the band jobs required and came home smelling of marijuana and beer.

Musicians like Dave didn't have to spend money on drugs and alcohol. People bought it for them, like an offering. They were the artistic gods of modern society and accepted, for the most part, their roles and gifts graciously. Unfortunately, it's this generosity that often leads to their downfall.

Brian was constantly hungry and I was constantly tired, but things were all right for awhile. As I look back, I realize that Dave was as ill-equipped for parenthood as I was. In no way was he prepared for the responsibility of a wife and baby, a daunting load even for those who had planned their lives in this fashion. He had dropped out of high school like I had done originally and possessed no real marketable skills except for music. But life went on and I found pleasure and comfort just looking into my baby's eyes and watching him grow. There was a feeling of reassurance when I held him, and I was at peace with the world and life, at least temporarily.

As much as I loved Dave, I was not sure I had done the right thing by marrying him, but it seemed like a good idea at the time. As time passed, however, it felt like we were growing apart instead of together. He would come home late from playing music and I would gently try to wake him for his day job the next morning. Depending on how much he'd had to drink, he would either be civil or clench his pillow and curse angrily. I, in turn, would become anxious about the possibility of him becoming unemployed when we desperately needed the income.

For years, Dave had been the only guy for me even though we had both dated others. My other boyfriends were primarily to show Dave that he could be replaced. Over time, however, I realized that he couldn't be replaced in my heart. I came to depend on him for so much; he was my addiction.

Now he was also my husband and the father of my child. I felt tied to him in every way, and, while both of us were undeniably free spirits, we were both beginning to feel the constraints of obligation and the responsibilities of adulthood.

I withdrew. He grew short-tempered. I cried. He shouted. The tension mounted as the responsibilities increased. As a couple, we were a ticking time bomb.

One morning, I went in to wake him and a fist caught me by surprise, knocking me backward against the closet. He shoved me into one wall, then the other, leaving me stunned in a heap on the floor. The beating was quick and explosive, and I realized only later that he was still drunk from the night before. In shock, I left and went to Mom and Dad's, only to return after a month for a reconciliation.

When we got back together, he became increasingly hostile and unpredictable. Finances were always a problem and sometimes food was scarce.

One time when we were hungry, he went to buy eggs and milk with our last few dollars. As he returned, his temper flared. Angrily, he threw the food down from the porch. The precious milk ran through the grass and most of the eggs were broken. I gazed at the mess numbly. Even after all these years, the image of the broken eggs and milk is still with me. I think it was at that point that I knew the marriage was over. But I still tried to make it work.

The next incident happened at night. After an argument, amid shouting and cursing, he raised a hand to hit me. I ran into the yard and hid in some bushes. As I hid, I thought of my sweet infant lying in his crib at the other end of our home. Would he be in danger? I thought not but wasn't sure. I knew by then that people were capable of anything while under the influence of alcohol or drugs, and Dave was almost always under the influence.

I waited in the dark hoping he would have gone to bed, then sneaked back toward the door, opening it slowly. Suddenly the door slammed shut on my hand, which was halfway inside. I couldn't get it loose! I tried using the other hand for leverage, but it too only ended up wedged in the door while he pushed from the other side.

I tried talking to him, then screaming at him. He was leaning heavily on the other side of the door, where half of my hand was, as he began systematically lighting matches to my fingers. He pulled me inside, and the fight was on. By the end it looked as if a tornado had hit our home, and I was lying blindly whimpering on the floor where he had smashed my eyeglasses and ground them into the floor.

My hands were swollen to the size of softballs. But my baby was all right.

I had loved Dave with all my heart but he became another person during these alcohol-fueled rages – someone neither of us liked very much.

After that, I think we both knew it was over and I couldn't come back. That would not have been in anyone's best interest, nor would it have been socially acceptable. People would have thought I was crazy to go back.

We both regretted that it had come to that and were ashamed of ourselves. Incredibly, though, the love was still there.

I would always miss the other Dave whose soft voice, quick wit, confidence and beautiful brown eyes had enchanted me from the start.

I stayed in our mobile home while he lived elsewhere, but I had no money, other than what little he gave me. Not knowing what to do and with no plans for the future, I did nothing. Times got harder and harder.

Hoping for miracles, I tried to ignore the nagging worries, hid my fears and focused on my child as much as possible.

Things came to a head while Mom and Dad were away on vacation. It was March and still cold in Wisconsin. Our heat and electricity had been turned off and the only food in the house was a half-gone jar of baby food, some pickles and butter in the refrigerator. Bills were due, and I was penniless. At that time, I didn't know that there were programs to help people in my situation and that I was not alone.

Panicking, I berated myself for having gotten into this mess and now began to think I was a terrible mother. How could I have let things go this far? What should I do next? My son deserved better than this.

I still missed Dave and had mixed emotions about the impending divorce. My life was a disaster, and I was just barely functional. The one thing I felt I had done right in life was having Brian. Now everything felt all wrong.

Mom and Dad had raised me to be independent, and I already felt I had let them down, so it didn't occur to me to try and contact them to ask for help. They had no idea how bad things were.

In tears, I called a social service agency and put my almost-toddler son into temporary foster care. I honestly felt it would be the best thing for him. I couldn't take care of him. As they took him away, my heart broke and I wanted to die right then and there. My sweet, well-behaved, smart little boy with the extra long eyelashes, like his dad and me, was gone.

In the lonely, cold, dark house, even lonelier with him gone, I retreated to my bedroom and cried, as my mother had done in her depression so many years before.

Upon my parents' return, they were livid and shocked to find their only grandchild in the custody of the state. They immediately took responsibility for him, taking him home to their house to raise and wondered if their only daughter was truly a nutcase. Their daughter was wondering that herself. I moved in with them and let Dave have our home until he could no longer afford it either. Then we sold it.

At least Brian and I were together again, with Mom and Dad taking care of both of us.

Thinking more clearly now, I knew I was going to have to do something else with my life since I was responsible for another.

This is an awesome responsibility that is often taken too lightly. It was one that I was not prepared for and more responsibility than I had ever had. In my case, it now served as a supreme motivator.

Looking ahead, I weighed the possibilities. Perhaps I needed more education and a trade of some kind. I loved my parents but knew we couldn't live with them forever. Show business was not something one could count on with sporadic work and inconsistent paychecks.

Finally, I moved to Milwaukee to put some distance between Dave and me and began attending the Patricia Stevens Finishing and Career College but quickly realized it was not what I needed or wanted. Once again, I felt that I didn't fit in and quickly became disillusioned and bored with what I felt was a shallow curriculum, one that focused on poise, wardrobe and shorthand.

I found a babysitter, began playing music again on weekends and tried to figure out what to do next.

Undecided about so many things, I questioned my faith or lack thereof, listed my options, talked with friends and thought long and hard during those lonely nights with the wind whistling off Lake Michigan.

My son and I were living in a one-room studio apartment when the divorce was finalized. I had a court appointed attorney, Dave had none, and it was I who told the judge that my husband had a substance abuse problem and needed help.

I didn't ask for anything. Child support was put on hold until Dave could address his problems. I didn't know "hold" would be forever.

We came out of the courtroom and hugged each other tightly, a bittersweet embrace.

Dave had been a big part of my life for nearly a decade. I knew I would miss him.

Part 2
Utah

Chapter 6

Westward HO!

All along the southbound odyssey
The train pulls out at Kankakee
Rolls along past houses, farms and fields.
Passin' trains that have no names,
Freight yards full of old black men
And the graveyards of the rusted automobiles.

- City of New Orleans, Steve Goodman

I had never spent much time west of the Mississippi , but Utah was calling. I was afraid that if I stuck around, I would be lured back into the relationship with Dave. Besides, I had friends in the Beehive State. So, in 1981, not long after the divorce was final, my 2-year old son and I left Milwaukee via Amtrak one cold, snowy Wisconsin day.

I can still see the faces of my tearful mother and worried father as we boarded the train.

They waved as we pulled away. With a place to stay, good schools and hope for the future, I wanted to begin life anew and put the past behind me.

Headed for Orem, Utah, we changed cars at Union Station in Chicago and acquired our own cozy little sleeper berth with bunks. Chugging west through miles of farmland past rivers and small towns, I tried to enjoy the trip. Looking out at the prairies, I had a sense of excitement, mixed with determination and some apprehension about our new life ahead. I had never been this far from home and wondered what was in store for us.

Watching the terrain turn from lush green to brown and gray as we headed further west, I was planning to do whatever was necessary in order to make a decent life for this little boy. I hoped that might mean finding a nice man to marry or at least more education so I could get a decent, steady job that wasn't in a bar or nightclub.

Little Brian was good-natured and cooperative, as usual. As we passed through the stockyards in Omaha, Neb., my precocious child, upon seeing the thousands of cattle, declared "There must be...25 cows out there!" That was the biggest number he knew at the time.

The trip was just long enough for me to gather my thoughts, prepare mentally and leave behind the remnants of my life in Wisconsin. My adventure was just beginning and from the train, the sight of the Mormon temple in Salt Lake City lit up at night was one of the most beautiful I had ever seen.

After a short stay with my friends, I soon found a small apartment in Provo and got acquainted with the public welfare services and food stamp offices. Help was available. Maybe we could make it.

I didn't have a car, television or a telephone and very few belongings but perhaps we didn't need much.

Decorating my tiny apartment the best I could, I made appointments at nearby Brigham Young University, where I hoped to further my education. There was much paperwork and many problems, but at least I was trying to do something constructive.

The beauty and scope of the Wasatch Mountains was impressive. Bordered by Mount Timpanogos to the east and Utah Lake to the west, this area, called the Wasatch Front, included Ogden, Salt Lake City and Provo and at the time was where 80 percent of all Utah residents lived. I was amazed to see snow on the mountaintops in July.

Settling in, I made friends with a few neighbors, almost all young newlyweds, some with babies. I spent time with my son. I filled out government forms, applied for everything possible and tried to remain optimistic about the future. Mom and Dad came to visit but still, I was lonely and Utah wasn't turning out to be quite what I'd hoped it might be. These mountains inspired awe and thoughts of grandeur as opposed to the friendly mountains of East Tennessee.

Single parents were not the norm in "Happy Valley" as some called the area, known for its idealistic and traditional views of family.

One neighbor told me there was another young divorcee in the neighborhood and that I should meet her. She wasn't sure, but thought her name was Rachelle and that she had two small sons.

"Great," I said. "Point her out to me sometime."

One day, slightly bored and discouraged, sitting on the step of my apartment while my son napped, I saw a rather frazzled-looking woman trudging slowly up the hill on the other side of the street. She was pulling a wagon loaded with bags and two little boys. Instantly, I knew this was the other single mom in the area.

"Hi! Are you Rachelle?" I yelled, jumping to my feet and heading in their direction.

She looked startled and wary as I ran over to introduce myself.

"I'm new around here," I continued, without waiting for an answer. "I live right over there, across the street next to the Hamby's and Taylor's… I haven't been here very long and was told there was another single mom in the neighborhood with some little boys – I have a little boy myself – and just thought you might be her since I've met almost everyone else..." I rattled on breathlessly.

"Well, I guess I am, at that," she said, still wondering who this crazy stranger was, chattering away on the sidewalk. "Where are you from?" she asked. Very few in the neighborhood were actually *from* Provo.

"Wisconsin. How about you?"

"North Dakota, with a little Montana thrown in"

Divorced single moms from the Midwest living in a sea of fresh, virginal, idealistic BYU students have a lot in common and a lot to talk about. Once again, like with Jo Ann, the keen sense of bonding and sisterhood came to my rescue, and Rachelle and I became inseparable. We were closer than sisters.

This friendship was my saving grace. Currently in nursing school, Rachelle, serious and studious, was a complete contrast to my bubbly impulsiveness. She had been through far worse than I, with two small mouths to feed and remained calm and positive in the face of my negative misgivings.

Devout in her religious beliefs, she was also earthy, practical and had a delightful sense of humor.

I helped her with homework and took a correspondence course from Brigham Young University. She helped me learn my way around town and campus. We babysat each other's kids, ate at each other's homes and talked endlessly. We overlooked each other's shortcomings and foibles with far more grace than most family members would have and supported each other.

It was she who first took me up into the mountains surrounding Provo, loading our kids into her little car one day. Driving past Bridal Veil Falls, up behind Mount Timpanogos to a hidden creek that shone in the sunlight, I saw a rainbow and felt a sense of admiration for the majesty of this rugged and beautiful land. I also began to feel more than a glimmer of hope for the future.

It was to Rachelle that I poured out my hopes, fears and dreams, past, present and future. Together we took our kids shopping and for pizza, an excuse for us to pig-out and enjoy the carnival-like atmosphere of the child-oriented pizza parlor. We both had boyfriends at the same time and neither relationship worked out. We discussed faith and reality and education and men and God. We shared secrets, laughter and tears and kept each other grounded in friendship.

Jo Ann, my dear friend from adolescence, and I had grown apart over the years. Miles, time and experiences separated us. But Rachelle and I bonded over everyday issues, intellect and our children. When one was down, the other cheered her up. When one was sick, the other made her well. We would walk to BYU dances and social events. We went out to eat, to parks and entertained our three kids. We shopped for groceries as one unit although we had separate apartments. I showed Rachelle how to use makeup more effectively, and she showed me Scriptures.

"You look beautiful," I assured her one day as she was getting ready to go somewhere.

"I can't look beautiful, I'm from North Dakota – remember?" she laughed.

Brigham Young, where Rachelle was attending school, had been my first choice in colleges, but my grades were not very good. My school track record was, in fact, miserable. I also found out that the University of Utah, 40 miles away in Salt Lake City, was on a quarter system, which appealed to me. I thought it might mean I could graduate faster.

Visiting Salt Lake with Rachelle and her friends, I enrolled at the "U," applying for all the financial aid for which I was eligible.

Before classes began, I went back to Wisconsin to visit, planning to leave Brian with Mom and Dad again temporarily while I began my studies. In Milwaukee, I was scheduled to have yet another in a long series of ear surgeries before heading back to start classes.

With Brian at Mom and Dad's, I had already made arrangements to stay with a young couple who lived in my former apartment building in Milwaukee.

While visiting old bandmates at a nightclub that evening, I was out late. I'll never know if I beat the young couple home, if they were gone or just didn't hear the doorbell buzzer, but I couldn't arouse them when I got back. Standing in the glass foyer of the building on the lower east side of Milwaukee, laying on the buzzer for minutes at a time with 3 a.m. rapidly approaching, I began feeling uneasy and nervous.

I thought I remembered hearing that there was a women's shelter somewhere in the area, so I called a crisis line from a phone booth around the block to see if I could find out where it was. Just as I anxiously gave my location to the woman at the other end of the line, something bumped into me and I screamed.

A man's arm quickly reached across in front of my face, hanging up the phone.

The tall, dark, wild-eyed stranger had a rather large gun stuck in my ribs. He had a hunted look about him and whispered through clenched teeth that he was going to kill me.

At first, gripped with fear, I couldn't talk. He half pushed me toward the sidewalk, still holding me tightly. I stumbled. Finding my footing and voice, I looked directly at him and forced a calmness I didn't feel. I asked him point blank what he wanted, which only seemed to confuse and infuriate him.

Walking me to a nearby car at gunpoint, he momentarily couldn't seem to decide which of us should drive the vehicle. The gun was trained on me the entire time, and my captor became more agitated by the second.

He finally decided to drive. As I was sitting in the passenger seat he ordered me to duck down as he hit me repeatedly with the butt of the gun. Twice, he held the gun to my head and cocked it but continued to drive.

Now bleeding profusely, I dimly thought of jumping from the moving car and began to feel around for a door handle only to find nothing but wires. Terrified, I began to suspect that I might not live to raise my son. I was thinking how mad my parents would be to hear of my murder.

My captor, angrier than ever with me for bleeding all over his car, seemed at once desperate, incoherent and confused. I vaguely remember hearing sirens approaching.

Looking back, I suspect the woman on the other end of the telephone that night knew a scream and a dead phone at that hour from a young woman at that location could only mean trouble and called the police. The closer the sirens grew, the more disoriented my captor seemed to become.

Without a doubt, I knew I was now going to die. Thoughts of what I had left undone and regrets flashed through my mind. I wondered if this was truly God's plan for me. Strangely, I also wondered what this man's life had been like to instill such hatred toward a stranger. In a weird way, I felt sorry for him.

My vision was clouded now by the blood in my eyes, and I gave in to what I thought was my inevitable demise. Slouching to the side in the seat, still trying to ward off the blows from the gun, I mourned inwardly for my little boy, who would now have to grow up without his mother and I prayed… silently and fervently. From somewhere within, I had the feeling that if I could call out loud to the Creator, the Almighty, all would be well. If only I could form the words...

Ultimately uttering a feeble "Dear God," somehow within minutes I was out of the car, but I still don't know how. I found myself in the middle of Prospect Avenue at 4 a.m., bleeding and terrified. Thinking the man would return to finish the job and kill me for sure, I ran to the first doorway I saw.

This was a former hotel that had been converted into a condominium with a clerk or attendant just beyond the door. Like the entrance at my old building, it had two sets of glass doors, the first set open, the second set locked with a doorbell on the wall in between. Someone on the other side would have access to a buzzer for admittance to the inner lobby.

After entering the outside set of doors, standing in the tiny vestibule, I rang the bell and pounded loudly on the second glass door, then shouted for help, still afraid my abductor would return. I rattled the handles, then screamed. Covered in blood, I was very visible to the man who sat behind a desk, looked at me and did nothing.

Eventually realizing he was not going to help me and beginning to lose consciousness, I made my way to the next building, where it too had two doors and a set of buzzers inside the entrance. I made it through the first door and pressed all the buttons, two at a time. Fortune was with me as someone buzzed me in without asking my identity. I began knocking at the first door and when a young woman answered I asked if she could please call an ambulance, collapsing on her floor.

Waking up in the emergency room, I was still terrified. Police were everywhere. Stitches were required and they had to cut some of my hair, but I was alive. I went straight from the emergency room to another hospital where I was scheduled to have the ear surgery. I don't remember much about either place.

While I recovered, detectives showed me pictures of the possible perpetrator. Some looked familiar, but I never could be sure and found out much later that an eyewitness identification is not always reliable anyway.

Friends came to visit me in the hospital where they later said they hadn't recognized me because I was so swollen, bruised and battered.

On August 27, 1981, The Milwaukee Journal ran a front-page story on the "big city apathy" shown by the clerk at the hotel who wouldn't help me. His reason for not helping a lone, disheveled woman covered in blood and screaming, pounding desperately on his door, was that I "appeared drunk."

Also on the front page of that same newspaper there was a small article about a woman's body that was found at a construction site. I later asked a detective if it was in any way connected to my experience.

Avoiding my query as long as possible, one of them finally told me that they thought the "guy didn't finish the job" with me so went on to someone else. He didn't tell me any more and I didn't ask, but I dreamed of that woman for a long time.

Chapter 7

Shoulder to the wheel

Eastbound and down, loaded up and truckin'
Ah we gonna do what they say can't be done
We've got a long way to go, and a short time to get there
I'm eastbound, just watch old Bandit run.

- Eastbound and Down from Smoky and the Bandit, Jerry Reed

I flew back to Utah with bruises and stitches, and Rachelle became my therapist. I had several experiences where my mind seemed to go blank, remembering nothing, even my own name. These were triggered by circumstances similar to my abduction in Milwaukee - out alone at night, seeing a certain make or color car or seeing a tall, slender African-American man coming directly toward me. Luckily, there weren't many of these episodes and they ceased within months.

I never knew if my assailant was caught.

Putting Milwaukee behind me, I immediately focused on school. The sooner I got some sort of degree, the sooner I could get Brian back from his loving grandparents, where he stayed temporarily while I got my act together. I decided to buckle down and get a college degree, no matter what it took.

Not knowing any better, I enrolled for 20 credits that first quarter. Twelve was considered full time. It would only be several days a week, including night classes.

Still with no transportation or phone, on school days I caught an early Greyhound bus from Provo to downtown Salt Lake City, walked or caught a city bus up the hill to the University of Utah campus, attended classes, then went back down the hill and caught a very late bus back after my night classes ended. Arriving in Provo in the wee hours of the morning, I walked back to my little apartment and fell asleep, exhausted.

Since it was not long after my experience in Milwaukee, on several occasions as I walked or waited for a ride or a bus after dark in Salt Lake City, I found myself uneasily withdrawing to the shadows of a bush or alcove on the outside of a building, wanting to hide. Haunted by a creeping feeling of paranoia and impending danger, I was on the verge of what I now know to be a panic attack, but with time it abated. I also had a few cognitive problems that arose after this incident, but they too disappeared over time.

I didn't feel threatened in any way in Provo, but I wore out the soles of my shoes at a ridiculous rate during that time.

Eventually falling in love with the University of Utah campus, I finally moved from Provo to Salt Lake City. After bringing Brian from his grandparents home in Wisconsin to a tiny, upstairs studio apartment, we rode the city bus to his day care center in the morning while I trudged across campus from class to class or studied for much of the day.

When we took the bus home again in the evening, I was often carrying my book bag, diaper bag and purse in one hand and my tired toddler in the other. It made for a long day.

Staples were oatmeal, peanut butter and macaroni. I didn't have much time or money to devote to meals. We both slept on a single rollaway cot. I liked this cot because it had a lightweight aluminum, fold-down, imitation brass headboard, my only luxury. Dad had gotten it for me while I was still in Wisconsin.

Our first several apartments were very cramped and very temporary, but I kept them clean and stocked with a few toys. Many moves later, the two of us got into student family housing, a far better situation than before.

Its clean, white cinder block walls offered us separate bedrooms and a playground full of children. Our lives were structured around the academic calendar. Sometimes Brian would stay with me and sometimes he would stay with his grandparents during the school quarter.

Much to my own surprise, I did well in my studies. I hadn't chosen a major but stayed actively involved in theater and now became involved in the world of cinema.

While still living at home in Wisconsin with my dreams of stardom, I had developed a fascination with film-making and drove to Dubuque, Iowa, one evening to watch a Sylvester Stallone movie being filmed on location.

Upon meeting him in person, I thought he looked rather like Elvis Presley - not that I had ever actually met the King of rock 'n' roll.

I was thrilled to shake the hand of the great director Norman Jewison and watched into the night as the klieg lights lit up the street. I saw them set up dollies with consideration given to camera angles and chatted with production assistants about technicalities.

The movie, *F.I.S.T.*, was not a blockbuster, but I was spellbound by the process.

Utah, being a right-to-work state with an endless variety of scenery had always been a viable resource for filmmakers of all kinds. They had a very active film commission, a branch of economic development designed to promote and facilitate filmmaking throughout the state.

Many early westerns had been shot in and around Moab, with its red bluffs, rugged terrain and brilliant sunsets. In fact, this tiny town had its own film commission.

Many commercials and television shows had been filmed in and around Salt Lake City, and it was fairly easy to get work for a day or two as an extra or be hired for a non-speaking role.

My earlier Oscar-winning dreams had been dormant since I had become a mother, but that didn't mean they had disappeared. I had enjoyed appearing in several movies and small screen projects by now, including regional commercials.

Actually, shooting movies was a rather repetitive process and often quite boring for actors on the set waiting for their call. We often waited for hours as the crew worked out lighting or logistics problems or we waited for an airplane to fly out of the camera frame. Still, I was enchanted with the business and was able to make a little money that way.

I hadn't been in Salt Lake City very long when I became involved in what was then called the United States Film & Video Festival. Receiving college credit as an independent study project, I jumped at the chance to learn more and rub elbows with industry professionals.

Volunteers and students like me were encouraged to go to the different seminars and activities. Thus, January of 1982 found me shivering with excitement and cold in the ski town of Park City, soaking up the wisdom of Brandon Tartikoff, Hal Linden, Roger Ebert, Joe Dante, Larry Schiller, Lee Grant, Judd Hirsch, Mike Medavoy and others in the business.

Trying to learn everything I could, I conscientiously went from one workshop to another and from one seminar to the next. A friend told me later that it seemed as if I were everywhere taking notes.

I was cold because the only boots I had leaked, my secondhand parka wouldn't zip, I had no hat or gloves, and there was snow everywhere.

High above Salt Lake, Park City was then a laid-back old silver mining town that became a bustling ski center in the winter. As I shivered my way through another event, I noticed one gentleman who seemed to be watching me intently. Later that day he introduced himself as John Earle, with the Utah Film Commission.

He had indeed been watching me, he admitted, and wondered who I was. I told him I was a nobody, just a student who was interested in films, and our casual encounter turned into an hour-long conversation about the industry, the film commission and more.

We ate lunch and established a friendship based on our mutual love of movie making. He was a delightful, interesting man and offered me a job when I got through with my studies.

I kept in touch with him periodically, to let him know how school was going and he let me know how the movie business was going. I fully intended to hold him to his word when I graduated. My future seemed secure. He also became instrumental in letting me know who might have a small role for me or when bit parts might be available for movies or television shows that were being shot in the area.

By 1984, Robert Redford's Sundance Institute, a nonprofit organization dedicated to providing support for independent filmmakers, was managing the festival. I was serving as an intern doing clerical work and critiquing scripts.

One day, dressed in my perpetual student grunge, with shoes untied, hair askew, no makeup, one earring missing and an ink smudge under my left eye, I was making reams of copies.

With stacks of papers in both arms, several sheets stuck in my pursed lips, I smelled like toner and glass cleaner and was in my usual hurry. Quickly turning from the cubbyhole where the copier was located, I ran smack into someone, scattering most of my papers except the ones in my mouth. I didn't attend mainstream movies much, but I looked up into the unmistakable eyes of a somewhat amused Robert Redford. I had met celebrities before but usually tried to leave a better impression.

The festival has now evolved into the Sundance Film Festival. It is still held in Park City and is one of the most unique, celebrated and best-attended events of its kind today. For me back then it held hope, education and a promise of a future. Nevertheless, I was still leading the life of a starving student. Nothing was easy.

I struggled financially. There was tuition and textbooks and activity fees and bus fare and so many other expenses. In addition to financial aid and work-study jobs, I also took out student loans. I didn't want to ask my parents for anything, but they helped me some and I almost always went home to Wisconsin on breaks from school.

Mom sometimes tucked a $10 or $20 in her letters and cards whenever she could, which was often what made the difference in whether or not I could eat lunch the next day.

My social life was almost nonexistent, and I missed my family. Moving from a relatively small Midwestern town to Salt Lake had been like moving from Mars to Jupiter. It was a big city with its own peculiar quirks and personality. The culture in Utah was very different than what I was used to back home.

In Utah, like in Rome, the dominant religion permeated everything. Even if you were a member of that religion, it could be cloying. The dominant religion in Wisconsin, as far as I could tell, had been beer and the Green Bay Packers.

The idiosyncrasies, the language, the commonalities the natives took for granted - all were new to an outsider. Rachelle was still in Provo and I missed her too. I was homesick often. Sometimes I was homesick for Tennessee and longed for those friendly mountains.

Whenever Brian wasn't with me I knew he was in good hands, but I missed him very much. I felt like I didn't deserve this beautiful child until I could provide a decent life for him. I wrote letters and called him often when he was in Wisconsin. When he was with me, I sometimes had no baby sitter and after he got older, he stayed alone for the hours I was in class or working. He became a latchkey kid at a very young age, letting himself in after school.

I wondered if things would ever get any better or easier for us as I trudged up the hill to class, late again after trying unsuccessfully to catch a ride.

One cold winter night, my mother was visiting and stayed with Brian while I went to class. Afterward, still without transportation, I tried to find a shortcut walking home to the housing complex.

I cut across a field, over a ditch and through Veteran's Administration hospital property and parking lots only to come up against a chain-link fence that seemed to have no end.

Home was in sight, just beyond my reach, beckoning. Tired, bedraggled and disgusted, I looked up and eyed the barrier I considered to be my adversary, the one thing that was between me, my family and a warm, comfortable bed.

"What the hell," I said as I strapped on my heavy backpack tightly and began to scale the fence that had stopped me cold.

At the top, gingerly straddling the chain-link squares with pigeon-toed feet, I balanced precariously as the weight of the heavy backpack shifted, pulling me to one side. Arms flailing but still balancing, I took it off, flinging it to the ground on the other side of the fence as I felt the top button of my jeans pop. Trying to avoid the sharp barbs on the wires at the top, I maneuvered my right foot into a better toehold, only to wrench my back in the process.

"Now, if only I could swing the left foot over and around...." I thought.

But the left foot was stuck. My shoe was wedged tightly into one of the squares at an angle that prevented it from going anywhere. I briefly had visions of myself stuck there until daylight when, hopefully, someone in the distant parking lot would notice me. Feeling very foolish, however, I wasn't sure I wanted anyone to notice me.

After berating myself for getting into this mess, I managed to back-track and wriggle the shoe loose, then come forward again. I had come this far already, I reasoned. My clothes were now torn, my ankle scratched and my right hand bleeding. Most of me was now on the desired side of the fence, but I couldn't figure out how to get down without completely tearing my coat, which was hopelessly hooked onto a sharp point on the wrong side of the fence. Straining to reach it, I scratched my other arm and ripped the rest of my button-front pants. I could feel one of the buttons lodged in between my underwear and left hip.

Now beside myself with frustration and disgust, my epithets and curses turned the still, night air blue.

"If only I had taken off the coat and thrown it with the backpack..." I moaned inwardly.

Finally deciding I could get another coat and that this one could be ripped to shreds for all I cared, I decided to jump. I looked down, braced myself, twisted and pushed away...to no avail. The coat was stronger than I thought and its thick material held fast as I hung suspended at an odd angle with the coat collar above the back left side of my head. The taut sleeves immobilized my arms and the rest of my clothes were bunched up around my arm pits except for my now loose pants, which began to fall down.

"Now what?" I thought to myself as my feet dangled in midair. I kicked at the fence, wriggled and writhed, pants inching lower with each movement.

In desperation, I finally angled my shoulders, straightened my arms up and back, gave a mighty push with my feet and landed on the ground with a thud. My coat still hung like a scarecrow in the moonlight.

Picking myself up, I mustered what dignity I could, pulled up my pants and found my backpack, the contents of which had scattered upon impact. Then I headed for home, but not before turning and giving a bitter, battle-weary middle finger to my nemesis, the fence. The jacket may be there yet.

⁂

Eventually I was able to buy an old clunker of a car that Brian, for some unknown reason, christened "Pinocchio." Rachelle had by now moved to Salt Lake City and into student housing. We were neighbors. However, she had become involved with a man whom she soon married. I was envious and didn't get to see her as much as I used to.

I clipped coupons, shopped at thrift stores and hoarded pennies. I found a second job and had to budget my time as carefully as I did my money.

The stress took its toll on me and classes were becoming harder. I began feeling burnt out, alone and desperate. Sometimes I would go to a local nightclub where they had a jam session on Sunday nights and played music. It was relaxing for me and I was paid a little, but I still had no real social life.

Bands offered me jobs playing music but I wanted to concentrate on school. I began dating sporadically, but never had much time. I was also scared of relationships after my disastrous marriage. However, at one of these jam sessions, I met Luke, a tall, dark, lanky harmonica player who sang country music the way it ought to be sung. We clicked onstage and the chemistry was like magic. Sweeping me off my feet in a whirlwind romance, I was probably easy prey. Lonely and distracted by school, finances and motherhood, I was also hungry for attention and affection.

Luke seemed to think I had connections in the music business and wanted us to "follow our dreams." He wanted to leave Utah, and it didn't take much to push me in that direction as well.

Within weeks Brian, Luke and I were headed to Wisconsin in "Pinocchio" as a family to put together a band. We took what possessions we could fit in the car and left everything else behind, leaving Rachelle to call the movers.

Once back home in Wisconsin, the band we assembled again became one of the best country bands in the area and received a lot of attention, much like Tumbleweed Rock.

Luke was a colorful character and Clark, who had a day job and was now married to my old friend Jo Ann, was again on lead guitar. I played keyboard, sang back-up vocals, auditioned other musicians, wrote press releases, managed and booked us.

I also managed Luke, who seemed to drink an awful lot of beer. I hadn't noticed this before. He didn't get mean, however, and was at times a rather humorous drunk. He didn't seem to want to do anything, however, except drink beer and play music.

We didn't talk much and shared even less by way of life experiences.

I realized that we had very little in common and I really hadn't known him very long. Perhaps I had made another mistake?

Brian stayed at Mom and Dad's a lot. I stayed busy, and as the band became more and more successful, Luke grew more and more distant, and drank more and more beer. He was never abusive but became increasingly withdrawn and I had the feeling that something just wasn't right.

One day I came home to our small apartment and found strange pictures, furnishings, dishes and clothes strewn about. There was jewelry and a comforter on the bed that I didn't recognize. A new dish drainer was near the sink. Puzzled, I tracked Luke down, asking about the items. After some initial hemming and hawing, he told me they belonged to Sandy, who then appeared at his side.

It seems that he had sent for an old girlfriend from Utah.

We had been having problems, but I sure hadn't expected this. I also found out later that he was still married to yet another woman. Feeling foolish, hurt and used, I didn't grieve long over Luke. Deciding he wasn't worth much heartache and I hadn't invested that much time in the relationship, I was over it.

Perhaps the best thing to do was to cut my losses and move on, dissolving the band and heading back out West. I wanted to put the Luke episode behind me.

❧

Trying to pick up where I left off back in Salt Lake City, Brian and I once again moved into student housing and I contacted John Earle. He was always glad to hear from me, and as usual, was upbeat and positive.

With renewed determination and resolve, I plunged into my studies.

This time, I didn't isolate myself quite as much. I dated several truly nice men and even had extended relationships. I will never forget Jalal, Mitch and Gino. Through them, I discovered new cultures and experienced emotional growth. I just couldn't bring myself to commit to romance or marriage.

Through my studies, I learned discipline, organization and critical thinking skills. I experienced intellectual growth. I also began to develop objectivity, maturity and confidence from within.

Rachelle was now expecting another child but had left her husband and moved back home to North Dakota. However, I soon discovered several other single mothers living in our complex who were attending school.

The nontraditional student was a new trend in Utah in the '80s. The University of Utah was progressive enough to recognize a Single Parent Student Association, for which I briefly became the volunteer acting director.

We all bonded and became an informal support system, commiserating about sick children, men, exams and finances, or the lack thereof.

I worked at the on-campus day care Brian now attended, was a receptionist for University Career Services and became chairperson of a four-day, campus-wide celebration of spring known as Mayfest '85.

I took extra credit assignments and attended classes that were not required.

I did everything I could think of that would look good on my future resume. Work-study jobs were my bread and butter, but I still played music on occasion and received some government assistance so money was not quite so tight.

I had written several songs during this time, primarily as an emotional outlet. The owner of one of the local clubs recorded three of them. I sent Mom and Dad a copy of this recording which they entered into a Kentucky Fried Chicken songwriting contest without my knowledge.

Imagine my surprise when I received a call from a Wisconsin radio station asking to interview the grand prize winner!

The winning entry had been inspired by a poem Dave had written for me long before, which I still kept in a box of precious mementos. Yes, I still missed him.

I granted the interview and was thrilled but was determined not to be seduced by music – or affairs of the heart – and stuck to my goal of becoming an over-achieving, briefcase-toting, dressed-for-success career gal with a decent, regular paycheck and benefits, hopefully working for the film commission. Besides, the prizes involved were minimal.

During this time national news was breaking from Tennessee. A friend had called to tell me that my dad was in trouble and I should turn on the evening news quickly.

She had met my parents previously and had seen the TV footage earlier that day. Puzzled, I turned on the channel and laughed. I called to reassure her that it was not my father. A man named Jake Dutcher, head of a banking empire and from the same county in Tennessee as my father, had been indicted for bank fraud. Sharing the same last name as my father, being from Tennessee and even resembling each other a bit, I could understand her concern.

Folks tell me that everyone from a small southern county who share the same surname are usually related, but I had never met Mr. Dutcher and he didn't come to our family reunions. A cousin worked for him once and Dad remembered that Jake's father owned a general store but that was about as close as we got to the handsome, flamboyant millionaire.

We had all heard of him because of his extravagant wealth, his unsuccessful bid for governor and his pivotal role in getting the 1982 World's Fair held in Knoxville, Tenn. We could possibly have been related. We all knew he was head of a financial institution but had never claimed him as kin and he had never claimed us. Later, however, this scenario would play a big role in our lives.

Chapter 8

My other car is a Pinto, the ring

But I'm strong
Strong enough to carry him
He ain't heavy, he's my brother.

- He Ain't Heavy, He's my Brother, the Hollies

Over time I grew to love Utah. In spring, the sweet smell of the blossoms on the trees and the white-capped mountains began to feel like home, and I felt more at peace with myself than I ever had before.

Brian and I were in Salt Lake City for the floods that ravaged the town in 1983 and helped to sandbag the area. We made more friends and began visiting the city's attractions. One year we enrolled in a beginner's downhill ski class sponsored by a local newspaper, and I later tried cross-country skiing.

We visited family friends in Moab, marveling at the vast expanse of land beyond Dead Horse Point. It looked like a miniature Grand Canyon. I loved the rugged canyon lands, arches and red cliffs.

We traveled to other parts of the West when I played music and I was in awe of the wide-open spaces as well as the vivid blue sky, sense of history and ever-changing countryside. I enjoyed these trips, but school was still a priority.

Campus, with its dignified circle drive and homey student center, became a comfortable place. I taught Brian to do somersaults on the green university lawn and we attended family day at the Natural History Museum.

With female friends nearby, we saw each other through courtships, crises and classes. Still in the pre-computer era, however, there were many frustrations involving red tape, financial aid, registration, transportation and more. If my financial aid didn't come through in time, I would be forced to withdraw from classes. I realized that it would take me longer than four years to get a four-year degree and settled in for the duration.

Having already worked in the theater as an actress without any sort of degree, I decided a diploma wasn't a requirement for success in that particular field.

My major was going to be communication, which was a little broader but still fit into my plans to work for the film commission according to John Earle. However, the College of Communication was one of the most popular on campus. Their requirements were very stringent and becoming tougher. In an effort to curb grade inflation, a "C" grading standard was adapted, a class couldn't be repeated more than once and upon entering a classroom of well over a hundred, we were told that only a third of us would pass. For some reason, this made me all the more determined to be one of those who succeeded.

Accepted into the program, I found a voice through my professors, even as I quaked under their tutelage. An "A" on a paper from Dr. Sillars meant more to me than the proverbial pot of gold at the end of the rainbow. I minored in family and consumer studies thinking that I needed the child development knowledge to be a better mother.

I also minored in theater, my first love, and recreation, after taking a class in recreational therapy. I kept changing my mind about a major and became an education junkie. I wanted to learn everything.

I began to do free lance work in public relations and marketing, doing everything from writing press releases to on-site consultations.

Rachelle, a thousand miles away, was able to hire me briefly, bringing me to Fargo as a consultant. I was able to increase referrals for her agency by 600 percent through basic public relations and marketing techniques and had a great time seeing my old pal. She now had a beautiful baby daughter.

I got another work-study job at the Pioneer Memorial Theater as a publicist where I got free tickets to all the shows. Whenever I could, I still worked in music, films or television, sometimes missing one or two days of classes to be an extra in a movie or for a quick road trip with a band. I spent time in Colorado, Nevada, Wyoming - in short, the American West, with its vast, colorful scenery. Sometimes Brian was with me and sometimes not.

At one resort where my band appeared regularly, I began dating a man who came on strong. He wined and dined me, took me to his ancestral family home and gave every appearance of being genuinely interested and devoted. I was beginning to fall for him when I learned quite by accident that he and another man had a bet: that he could win my affections and have me in his bed within a certain time frame.

When I confronted him, he came clean and confessed. Any feelings I might have had for him were gone instantly, but I agreed to pretend and play along, letting the other man *think* we had been intimate. I even jokingly implied that he lacked as a lover! He won the rather substantial wager and split it with me. Calling sporadically for years afterward and professing real love, he begged for a second chance, regretting his initial actions, but I wasn't interested.

I learned that appearance counted in all relationships. Men were attracted to the earthy image of beauty and glamour that I was able to put on and take off professionally at will. Indeed, the songbird or rock 'n' roller onstage weekends bore no physical resemblance to the harried, frazzled, single mother who was a full-time student during the week. Blue jeans and torn sweatshirts were no match for evening gowns and glitter. Unruly hair was covered or sculpted with a full container of gel and make-up was theatrical for shows. The working student had little time for either.

Most of the men who were attracted to one had no interest in the other. Even friends who were forewarned literally recognized one persona but not the other. The transformation was sometimes truly shocking.

For this reason, I kept my two lives very separate. It was almost like having a dual identity. But, the two characters served their purpose. "Mousy Me" wouldn't have been seen under the bright lights onstage and certainly didn't add much to the show as far as visual appeal. "Barbie Doll Me" would never have gone over in academia. She wouldn't have been taken seriously.

When "Pinnochio" finally died and I was desperate for wheels, I bought a newer car, still very much a no-frills, basic 4-cylinder model, but in a little better shape.

When one is dependent on government programs, one also must share every change in circumstance and detail of one's life with the accountable agency. I told the food stamp office of my new acquisition and they told me that the newer automobile put me just over the limit to receive benefits. I would have to take it back if I still wanted their help.

I desperately needed reliable transportation and was devastated. Car shopping was an ordeal to begin with. Frustrated and in tears back at the car dealership, I told them honestly of my plight and wanted nothing to do with *any* car, afraid I might get into trouble. They tried to help find a solution but there were no older cars on the lot. They wondered if an automobile could be put into someone else's name, but I was at the end of my rope, ready to give up and walk home.

Without transportation, I felt without hope and sat in their waiting room totally dejected while they rescinded the original deal. I was grateful they were understanding and cooperative. Some of the employees were even trying to cheer me up, offering soft drinks and snacks. When they had me peek at a sleek 280ZX sports car that was still being detailed, I knew they were trying to humor me.

"Oh, it's beautiful. I could *never* get anything like that in a million years," I sniffed, red-eyed. "I probably wouldn't even know how to drive something that gorgeous," I joked lamely.

But the kind salesman and sympathetic dealership must have felt sorry for me because they offered to give me the silver two-seater with sunroofs for the same price as the other car. Insurance costs were not much different and Dad, my accomplice back in Wisconsin, had them put it in his name.

I used to look out the window at that car and marvel that I was actually driving something that flashy and sophisticated. The robotic feminine voice that told me my door was ajar or my fuel was low became my friend, and during times of high stress I could drive up into the mountains with Brian, leaving my worries and cares behind, in a ride that was actually fun to drive. With the sunroofs off and the stereo on, I felt free as a bird and the car reliably got me through the rest of my years of schooling in Utah, took me to gigs on the road and back home for the holidays. At some point, I was able to put it in my own name – and get off food stamps.

There were many challenges on a daily basis involved in trying to get an education and get ahead. My good-natured friend, neighbor and fellow student, Penny, who had three kids, often babysat Brian and became a trusted confidant. I also babysat for her children and we alternately gossiped and studied. But studying is harder with three kids than just one. Financial and logistical problems are greater as well and finally, burnt-out and driven by stress, she loaded up her kids and belongings one day, leaving for her home and family in Arizona, much like I had done with Luke.

She didn't know for sure where she would end up and I didn't hear from her again. I often wondered what had happened to her but had no idea where to look, and there were other pressing matters at hand.

My only brother Clark was just a couple of years younger than I. We shared not only parents but friends, interests and hobbies. Married now to my childhood friend Jo Ann, he worked on the railhead at the company where my father worked.

I had tormented him throughout the years, something I generally thought of as a big-sister privilege, duty and even responsibility. I was Lucy to his Linus. We had the usual fights and sibling rivalry.

He also tormented me, especially as he got older, but if anything had threatened either of us, one would probably have been the first to defend the other. One night a bully knocked out Clark's front teeth in a sucker punch at the skating rink, and I wanted to personally tear out the young man's eyeballs and hang him by the heels.

As children, we invented the game "Tumble-Bumble" where we tumbled around the floor in a circular fashion, round and round, chasing each other. We draped blankets over tables and chairs to make tents in the living room. We inspected new kittens, rode bikes and dissolved into laughter, privately imitating certain relatives and neighbors. We kept each other's youthful indiscretions a secret and discovered music together.

Clark, the model child, was the one who never caused trouble. I was the renegade. Always rebellious, I questioned authority and everything else. At one time I thought I never wanted children because they might turn out to be like me. In my teen years, both of my parents and I went at it tooth and nail. Of course, then we would tearfully make up, and I would find another way to test their patience and push the envelope.

Clark wasn't like that. He was quiet and sweet in the wake of a brash, aggressive big sister. He had friends and never did wrong - or at least didn't get caught at it. He and his friends were among the 14 kids stuffed in Mom and Dad's Corvair whom I drove around the Circuit.

He drank a little, like all of our contemporaries, and once I even saw him down an entire bottle of Southern Comfort, not realizing there was such a thing as alcohol poisoning at the time. He let me ride his mini-motorcycle through the fields in back of our house and didn't even get mad when I wrecked it once.

Sometimes I envied Clark's ability to never make waves and was very proud of his talent on guitar. He was bright and intelligent but not the studious or academic type. When he graduated from his small trail bike to a big, real motorcycle, I worried about him.

As a teenager, I sometimes felt like he thought he had something to prove, but that may have been because most of the kids he hung around with were older. He was the youngest member of Tumbleweed Rock.

I had been the pregnant maid of honor at Clark and Jo Ann's wedding and they lavished gifts upon Brian and me each birthday and Christmas. They were kind and supportive and both worked very hard at several jobs. We were not as close after I moved to Utah because we all led busy lives as adults but kept in touch by phone periodically.

One night when Clark called, our conversation seemed to not make sense, but, busy with my own life, I thought no more about it. He called soon after that and again sounded like he was talking nonsense. His tone left me uneasy and I knew something was wrong, but I didn't know what.

Sometimes when something troubled me, I would try to ignore it hoping it would go away or get better. This is what I did with those nagging thoughts of Clark: tucked them away in the back of my mind. I didn't know enough to deal with whatever it was. But something was indeed wrong.

In 1985, after eating Easter dinner with extended family at a Madison, Wis. restaurant, Clark came back to Mom and Dad's house along with everyone else. Celebrations were festive at our house. Family, friends and food were par for the course. This was no different; however, that evening Clark wouldn't sit anywhere near a window and didn't want Dad to either for some strange reason.

He displayed other somewhat unusual behavior throughout the evening, according to Mom and Dad, including pacing and staring at the door. In retrospect, his erratic actions, seemingly random references and words seemed even more ominous.

Mom tried not to think about the fact that Clark was becoming increasingly irrational as the evening wore on and she didn't know what to do about it. She and Dad just knew something was desperately wrong. It became as obvious as having a pink elephant in your living room and almost as impossible for them to ignore.

Their concern grew as Clark's unnerving behavior grew even stranger. The crowd dwindled as the night wore on, but still no one realized anything was wrong except Mom and Dad.

We found out later that Clark thought an imaginary enemy waited just outside. Clark believed the imaginary enemy wanted to kill him and his family. This was his reason for not wanting to be near a window. References to the Mafia, subversive military groups and Jake Dutcher entered his conversation, and he displayed more paranoid behavior.

Eventually, it became evident that he was not in touch with reality. It was as if he were living out a movie plot. Clark insisted on lying on the floor, listening at the threshold almost all night. Dad lay on the floor with Clark, trying to constantly reassure him that all was well, but Clark would still periodically get up to check out the windows and listen by the door to see if "they" were still there.

During the night, he told Dad he might have to run up to a friend's house to get a gun. (We'd never had any guns in our house.)

Later, Dad whispered to Mom, "...if I lose his confidence, we may all be in trouble..."

Clark was strong and had a black belt in martial arts. It was a very long night and a nightmare for Mom, Dad and Doris, my step-grandmother, who was then staying with them. Even she might have possibly come to feel that something was amiss, but quietly went to bed.

The next day Mom desperately sought help for her obviously troubled son, but by the end of the day Clark was in jail, Dad had a concussion and a local policeman who was a friend of the family was lucky to be alive.

While Mom was gone trying to find help, Dad had tried hard to maintain Clark's trust. However, when Dad called his employer to tell them he wasn't coming to work that day, Clark immediately become suspicious. Dad said later that he knew at that moment that he had lost him.

Clark ran to the back door where Dad tried to grab him in a bear hug to keep him from leaving, not knowing what would happen and fearing the worst. Clark got far enough away from him so he could land a blow, knocking Dad against a basement door, giving him a concussion and cutting his eye. Clark then ran next door to a neighbor asking to borrow a gun.

With no success there, he ran to another house that was locked and nobody was home.

Clark, caught in the unreality of a full-blown delusional state and in survival mode, thought he was now in a fight for his life. He ran to yet another neighbor's house where he dashed in, telling them who he was and that he needed a gun because there was trouble. The neighbor told him if there was trouble he should call the police, so my confused brother called the law as a defense against the imaginary enemies that were hunting him down.

Amid the cadre of officers to answer the call was Darryl Fox, a long-time family friend and one of Janesville's finest. Not quite knowing what they were dealing with yet, Darryl approached Clark, who by now thought the enemy was closing in. Not knowing whom he could or couldn't trust, Clark lunged for Darryl's gun, and a struggle ensued. The gun discharged through the ceiling, and the fight was on.

It took six to eight officers to subdue my little brother, who at that point thought that everyone was part of the plot. It was apparent that he had now lost all touch with reality and was deep into his own version of it.

After first being taken to jail, he was later taken to Mendota Mental Health Institute in Madison, Wis. for evaluation. He was then sent to the county hospital in Janesville, where he ultimately stayed for four months.

I was still in Utah and immediately turned to Rachelle, who by now, coincidentally, was a psychiatric R.N.

I don't know what our family would have done without her help and guidance from afar. My poor parents, along with Clark's wife Jo Ann were struggling with disbelief and confusion.

It's difficult to realize that the brain, like any other vital organ such as the liver, lungs or kidneys, can become ill and Clark was clearly in the throes of major psychosis. This was like something you see in movies or read about, but *it doesn't happen in your family.*

Psychosis does not take away from creativity, talent, intelligence or physical prowess. This was still my same sweet, talented, intelligent little brother, but he believed himself and everyone else he knew to be caught up in a web of conspiracy, violence, revenge and crime.

I flew back from Utah to see what I could do to help. By virtue of now being the most educated member of our immediate family, I was expected to have some answers. And I did, thanks to Rachelle.

While visiting Clark in the hospital, he seemed to be doing all right. I talked with the doctors, social workers and the legal team. They were trying to stabilize him, and he seemed quite normal… until he showed me the ring.

At some point in the past, Dad had given Clark a ring. It was costume jewelry and Dad never wore rings, afraid they would catch on a piece of equipment at work. He kept jewelry and some old coins, a wooden nickel and a few other assorted personal mementos in a small box of treasures that we kids liked to solemnly look at on occasion.

The black and white ring was in the shape of a chess piece and at some point, Dad had given it to Clark. This was the ring that had cut Dad's eye in the fracas. It had no special significance to Dad or to our family whatsoever.

However, it acquired a special, personal significance to Clark at some point, for reasons known only in his distorted mind.

I dimly recall seeing a movie or television show about organized crime where a certain ring signified power or was used as some sort of identification. Perhaps Clark had seen the same show.

Visiting with him now, I thought everything might be all right when he said

"They know everything now."

I was relieved to hear this because if doctors don't know what a patient is thinking, they can't know the extent of the psychosis. I had encouraged Clark to tell all, not to hold back.

"Yes, I've told them everything," said Clark.

"That's good," I said, still trying to be a reassuring big sister. "Do you feel all right now?" I asked, knowing that the feeling of sheer terror is real whether in a delusional state or based upon reality. The delusion, in fact, becomes the patient's reality.

"Well...at least somebody knows now" he replied. I thought he was talking about his illness. "They wanted to know about Dad," he said.

"What about Dad?" I asked slowly.

He had been talking and behaving rationally until now, and lowering his voice, he said, "They know all about him except for this..." And he pointed to the ring.

My eyes widened. "What about that...?" I asked.

"Don't you know about this?"

"No, tell me."

"Do you know about Jake?" he asked, again lowering his voice, referring to Jake Dutcher, who, for some reason had become a part of the plot.

As stated before, none of us had so much as ever met the man. Clark then gave me a look so full of meaning that I almost panicked.

At this point, I realized he was not rational at all yet. He was still wrapped in his delusion. That ring held some significance that only someone who had seen too many movies could understand. That ring had taken on a symbolism that was beyond description. That ring had become a focus for Clark's fictional reality.

Just then someone entered the room.

"You can tell me later," I whispered to Clark, and left soon after, racing to tell whomever I could that the medication wasn't working and he was still out of touch. No one else had realized it yet.

He thought he was playing some sort of survival game by playing along. But he had confided in me. I felt like a rat, but my brother's health and safety was all-important.

In psychosis, delusions are blended so completely with reality that often the delusional state will remain hidden. Under questioning, the person may well be able to give expected and correct answers and carry on a perfectly reasonable conversation, while at the same time still believing they are being interviewed by aliens, that they are the Messiah, or in Clark's case, that our Dad apparently was the Godfather.

Mental illness can be extremely hard on loved ones and those around the patient and it was horrible for Mom and Dad. Clark's original diagnosis was paranoid schizophrenia, although there may have been other disorders present too. It was particularly hard on my father, who didn't believe mental illness even existed and has trouble, like many others, understanding that the brain can and does malfunction.

Like many men his age, Dad has always maintained a mind-over-matter mentality. In Dad's world, the mind does not get sick, and if it does you can *will* yourself better and talk yourself out of it.

Unfortunately, research shows that more and more mental illness is found to have a physiological base, usually a chemical imbalance of some sort, therefore this reasoning would not work any more than it would for diabetes, heart disease or high blood pressure.

Perhaps with some afflictions, a strong spirit and positive thinking can make a big difference, but in Clark's case he was not aware that there was anything wrong to begin with. He thought he was the only one who knew the mob was out to get him and his family and that he needed to protect himself and everyone else.

Eventually, after dealing with hospitalization and the many side effects that often accompany psychotropic medication, the health care team arrived at a combination of drugs that stabilized Clark. To this day, he maintains a daily regimen of medications. He knows the consequences of being without it.

My parents still can't recall this part of their lives without becoming almost physically ill. Jo Ann, separated from Clark at the time of his breakdown, stuck with him throughout the ordeal and hospitalization but they divorced later after having a son.

Clark has dealt with the stigma and effects of mental illness admirably. He is now remarried, lives in the community and does well. Friendly, generous, kind and intelligent, he has accomplished a great deal and I am proud of him, especially knowing that often those with severe mental illness must remain institutionalized for life and can't function at all in society. My hat is off to him.

Chapter 9

Life on the Road

On the road again
Just can't wait to get on the road again
The life I love is makin' music with my friends
And I can't wait to get on the road again

\- *On the Road Again, Willie Nelson*

Back in Utah, I was again working in bands. I took occasional acting jobs and held day jobs, too. I played with a rock band called Gypsy Wind and wore a black tee-shirt emblazoned with the words "Rock Goddess" - a gift from the rest of the band.

I played country music with another band and opened for bigger names in some towns. I even did a short-lived piano bar/dining music venue. To be honest, when playing music, I was bored when I wasn't rock 'n' rollin. But country music was what paid the bills.

Fortunate enough to have a friend who owned a day spa, I worked there periodically and was allowed to use the tanning booths, facial machine and cosmetics. Born in Finland, her English was sometimes fractured but endearing, and she taught me much about the business of beauty. The Finnish Touch became my home away from home.

I still dated, but not seriously and moved to an apartment off-campus. Rachelle, now divorced and back in Salt Lake City, and I were roommates for a while, blending our kids again into one family.

One September, Sky Blue and the Ghost Riders, a band with whom I performed, had even been booked for the Arts Festival of the Canyonlands, spending a balmy evening on the banks of the Colorado River near Moab.

Sky Blue was really Wil Numkena, one of the most educated, gracious and talented men I had ever met and a full-blooded Hopi Indian. He had a government job during the day, but his music career had won him awards and taken him to Nashville in the past.

The band worked steadily, had no inclination toward excessive partying and got along well. I considered them to be like brothers and often took Brian with me on these music jobs.

Booked near Duchesne, Utah one Fourth of July weekend, Brian and I were out hiking behind the Native American resort where the band was performing. It looked for all the world like a scene from a John Wayne movie with a ghost town in the distance and the desert sun beating down.

The bleached earth with its slow rises and rugged brush summoned visions of desperadoes, stagecoaches and the old West with which I was enamored. Perhaps I'd seen too many movies. I half expected to see the silhouette of a befeathered native on horseback atop the ridge in the distance.

We hadn't been walking very long when I thought I heard the sound of distant drums. Could...? Could...Was it possible...? Could there be tom-toms in the air, or had my romantic dreams of the frontier driven me mad? No... there it was again! War cries! Was that chanting...? I was hearing things! Or was I? I sent Brian back to the swimming pool, where he wanted to be anyway. Yes, there it was again... the unmistakable sound of war drums! I had seen enough westerns to be sure of that! Perhaps I was having auditory hallucinations – *was* there such a thing?

I looked around incredulously and scanned the sky for smoke signals, finally racing back to the resort to find Sky and the rest of the band. In their room, I panted that I didn't think I could perform that night, that I may have heat stroke and quite possibly the western sun had driven me crazy. When pressed, I confessed that I thought I heard Indian drums out in back. Sky began laughing hysterically, to my surprise.

"You really *did* hear the sound of tom-toms and chants... There's a Pow Wow going on just over the hill there," he managed amid laughter.

"What's a Pow Wow?" I asked, still wild-eyed.

"It is a traditional Native American celebration of culture, attended by many. The festivities include dancing, music, crafts and food. They have them all over the country," he replied, still laughing.

We'd never had one in Janesville.

"Will...will they let white people in?" I hesitantly asked him.

With tears of mirth still in his eyes, he patiently told me that everyone was invited and the townspeople looked forward to it each year. Native Americans and others came from very far away to be part of this gathering. He said I should go and take Brian. It would be an educational experience.

We did go and it was one of the most memorable experiences of both of our lives. Amid the drums, chanting and throngs of Native Americans in full regalia, young Brian held my hand tightly and hesitantly asked if they were going to attack. They didn't. We ate Indian fry bread and bought feather necklaces and learned a lot about a beautiful and ancient culture. I understand there has even been a Pow Wow in Janesville now, too.

I performed at concerts, fairs, clubs, ballparks and rodeos, but the last venue was very dangerous for me.

My love for animals was always evident, but I was allergic to them.

Out of all my allergies, I was most allergic to horses. Being a city gal, it never really bothered me because I had no opportunity or desire to be around them. The few times I was, through friends or by accident, the result was disastrous! I couldn't even be downwind from these particular animals, and a family joke was that I couldn't watch horses on television without having a classic allergic reaction and asthma attack.

One time, playing music in a club, I became increasingly ill as the night wore on, coughing, wheezing, sneezing and unable to talk, much less sing. With tears running from my red, swollen, itchy eyes, I recognized this as an allergy. But we had played this particular club often in the past with no problem. I couldn't figure out what was different this time.

By the middle of the night, I was running outside to gulp air every break and knew I was heading for trouble. After our last break, toward the end of the night, our lead singer publicly welcomed all the "fine folks from the horse show" whom he had just met and I was out the door on my way to the hospital.

Another time with a different band, we were playing in Las Vegas. It was the first time I had ever been in a casino. There weren't any of those in Janesville either.

I didn't know gambling from hog farming and wasn't all that eager to learn, but our hosts gave each band member a roll of nickels to use on the slot machines as a courtesy.

My fellow band-mates took off and I watched as patrons systematically inserted their coins and stared at the machines.

At first, I decided I was going to hang on to my nickels. Money had been too hard to come by. But the people around me seemed so intense, it was like they were hypnotized by the face of the machine in front of them. I watched as a man filled a cup with quarters spewing from a spout. A woman methodically inserted coin after coin from stacks she had piled on the side of the machine. Another woman wore a bracelet of dice with a rabbits foot attached.

Gambling has gone digital now but in those days, there was actually a handle or lever you had to pull.

I wondered about this addictive fascination with luck and chance.

"What the hell," I thought, and put a nickel in the closest one. "I'll try it just this once. Then at least I can say I've done it," I thought.

To my surprise, the machine ejected a sizeable pile of nickels. I scooped them up and moved to another machine, repeating the process. This machine didn't give me any money so I moved on. There weren't very many people around at the moment and I was taking in everything, the opulence of the building, the oblivion of the players, the music in the background and the general atmosphere.

The place started filling up with people as I slowly put nickels in one machine and then another. Occasionally one would give me a few coins back. As I paused at one of the gaudy contraptions, tentatively feeding it my last few coins, a red light and siren like a police car went off on top of the machine.

In a panic, I quickly moved away from the offending and embarrassing situation, thinking I'd done wrong and broken something. Flashing red lights and a siren where I came from were *not* good news. I had no idea what I'd done but hoped nobody had seen me.

Walking quickly back through the lobby, I tried to act nonchalant, made my way to the restaurant and into the rest room. Eventually, I slunk back to our quarters and later told the guys what happened, thinking I must have broken a machine or the law. They looked at one another, then rushed out the door, grabbing my arm and running.

We raced toward the casino floor. They demanded to know WHICH MACHINE I had used. The slots all looked alike to me and I had disappeared for quite a while from the now crowded and unfamiliar gaming hall, so couldn't identify it for sure.

I thought they were turning me in for whatever I'd done. How was I supposed to know that a flashing red light and siren meant the player had won the jackpot? But it was too late. I didn't get any money.

Hard to believe I was that old and still that naive.

I later put together a show with a different band that was part music and part comedy, which we took to several different locations in Nevada. Sponsored by a chain of wedding chapels and women's clothing stores, I finally got to wear elegant ball gowns! I even got a few modeling jobs during this time period even though I was never the classic model type, physically.

I performed in several tribute shows and played with other bands, often filling in for absent performers.

A child of the '60s, who came of age in the early '70s, I was part of the Flower Power generation, but had experimented only minimally with the freedoms the Age of Aquarius offered.

After witnessing heartbreak, violence and destruction from alcohol and drug abuse, I made the decision that I would abstain, but few of my comrades seemed to agree with this philosophy. In fact, sex, drugs and rock and roll seemed to be the order of the day for many.

Certainly not everyone in show business buys into a life of excesses, decadence and debauchery, of course, but in many cases, my fellow actors and musicians did. Illegal substances and illicit liaisons were a way of life for some.

My own crazy out-of-control antics and behavior were kept onstage as part of my performance and where country music was concerned, I didn't believe you had to live Hank William's life in order to sing his songs. After a show, I preferred to go read and relax in my room and I didn't take Brian with me when I knew the company might be questionable. When raucous times interfered with my sleep, I turned over and slept on my one good ear, shutting out the noise.

Always, I was generously offered a hit, toke, line or drink when others indulged, and at times I think I inhaled enough second-hand marijuana smoke to get a contact high, but after a while, everyone knew where I stood on these matters.

I was not judgmental of those who did partake, however, and learned to turn a blind eye. So although I attended my share of backstage parties and had been privy to some hair-raising escapades at hotels and on tour busses, my walk on the wild side was that of a disinterested bystander; it was all around me, but I was unfazed and untouched. I wasn't even familiar with much of the drug-related jargon or paraphernalia of the day. Because I had no interest, I paid no attention.

My biggest vice was probably junk food.

Munching on some mini-donuts covered in powdered sugar one night at a club, I hurriedly came back from a break with some of the sugar apparently on my nose and upper lip. Vince, a hulking new, 6-foot-4, none-too-intelligent, bass guitar player and dedicated longtime user of a variety of recreational chemicals, bent over and looked at me closely. Unable to figure out what he was doing and unaware that I was wearing the sugar on my face, I was caught off guard when he said,

"*Wow*, man, like, I didn't know you did *blow*! Cool...."

I didn't know then that "doing blow" was a slang term for using cocaine and to him it looked like I'd had a nose full. I thought he was asking for a blow job (Slang term for oral sex, with which I *was* familiar but also didn't indulge), so I told him firmly that he needed to find sexual satisfaction elsewhere.

He just looked at me kind of funny, then walked away, scratching his head.

One of my last tours was with an up-and-coming vocalist out of Nashville, again taking now 11-year-old Brian. We played fairs and concerts in Colorado, Nevada and Wyoming again, as well as Idaho, California and Oregon.

We enjoyed the Cantaloupe Festival in Fallon, Nevada and saw a geyser in Bend, Oregon. We gazed at the performers in Circus-Circus and marveled at the lights of Vegas once more. I always tried to make these road trips as fun and enlightening as possible, almost like a vacation.

My favorite shows were always fairs, a smorgasbord of junk food and humanity. I always took extra time before the show and, if possible, the day after to sample the fun.

Stopped at the top of a Ferris wheel with Brian by my side, looking out on a Pacific sunset from a fairground in Ventura, Calif., I thought how very lucky I was to have been able to experience all of this. Living in the moment and observant of the larger picture, I was profoundly grateful that life had become easier – it had even become beautiful.

I was happy and looking forward to the future. I'd had to leave home, experience challenges and endure hardships to find true independence. I needed that independence to define myself and grow as a person. I no longer blamed my parents for who I was and accomplishments and experiences brought more confidence and self-esteem. Newfound maturity and a new positive attitude afforded some degree of inner peace.

There was still a shadow of restlessness within my spirit, however.

With college graduation finally in sight, I decided to contact John Earle again, whom I hadn't seen in quite a while. I had done well in school and with performing, largely due to my complete willingness to make an utter fool of myself on camera or on stage, but I was ready to jump full time into my career with the film commission.

I trusted this man. I thought of him as my mentor and had prepared diligently, guided by our sporadic conversations throughout the years. This had been the goal in the back of my mind as I chose classes and became involved in what extracurricular activities I could.

Preparing an official resume and the obligatory cover letter, I called John to warn him that they would be on their way and invite him to my graduation.

"Mr. Earle!" exclaimed the receptionist, like she didn't know who I was talking about. "When was the last time you talked with him?"

I told her it had been a while and gave my name again.

"Are you a friend of his?"

"Well, yes, I guess. More of a business acquaintance, maybe," I explained, wondering if he was out in the field taking pictures or on location somewhere.

"I am so sorry to tell you this but Mr. Earle passed away..."

"He... what? He d-died....???"

I was incredulous. The man was a picture of health as far as I knew, and still young. Of course, I hadn't actually seen him in a long time. She told me his obituary had appeared in the newspaper, but I didn't subscribe. That year the film festival had been dedicated to him, but I had not been involved.

Her voice droned on over the phone as my hopes for the future grew dimmer and dimmer. His replacement had never even heard of me. I felt like I had lost not only a good friend but a future as well.

Continuing my education long after I accumulated enough credits to graduate, I could probably have earned several degrees. Besides the academics required, I had classes in common medicines (very helpful), belly dance (not as helpful), and earned a certificate in "Clownology," offered through the theater department.

The latter introduced me to the fine art of making balloon animals, (something I never could quite get the hang of) and magic, which I took to instantly. I made a few bucks doing magic/clown shows for kids, and my Middle Eastern boyfriend appreciated my attempts at belly dance.

Almost five years of varying levels of improvisational theater classes helped me to learn to be flexible and creative, think on my feet, relax, be comfortable in my own skin and have fun.

I also had classes that opened my eyes to diversity, research and personal responsibility. I was introduced to critical analysis, theory and self-awareness.

The liberal arts based education I received in Utah had led me into realms I never knew existed - and my lessons hadn't always taken place in the classroom.

Upon my graduation, Mom and Dad, Clark and Jo Ann, my aunt, uncle and step grandmother from Wisconsin convened on the University of Utah campus. I knew they were all proud, but it seemed to me that there was a feeling of disbelief that one of their own had actually gotten a college degree. Higher education was an anomaly in our family.

One of my professors even came to the party afterward at my home, where I played the piano and we sang and celebrated as much as sober people from Wisconsin can.

My first real job after graduation was as National Public Relations Director for a retail franchise venture selling licensed sports apparel and memorabilia.

Now gainfully employed full-time, the state job-training people were proud of me because I was finally considered a success. I was no longer a drain on the public welfare program even though I was making barely more than minimum wage and given very little to do. In reality, I was the token female of the team. I became bored and kept looking for other opportunities.

It was around this time that I was recruited for a musical project called California-Oklahoma Country.

A wealthy San Diego businessman was looking for musicians from all over the country to form what he hoped would be a premiere 18-piece country-show band. A number of us were flown to San Diego where we were guests at a beautiful motel on the beach in La Jolla.

With a white limousine at our disposal, we were treated like royalty. Wined and dined, we were taken out on a yacht, shown the sights and ultimately taken into a studio. I loved every minute of it. After this initial get-together, we would at some point be called to Park City, Utah, where the backer of the project owned a great house, high on a mountain above the ski slopes. Park City was just up the road from me and a favorite spot of mine ever since the film festival, but others were from as far away as Ohio, Tennessee and New Jersey.

Single people were to reside at the backer's huge, lavish residence and everything would be provided. Those with families, like me, were to live in a condominium on the main street with all expenses paid, an allowance for food and a salary. All that was required of us was to play and write music.

I kept asking, "What's the catch?" But there was no catch. This man just wanted to be involved with the music industry, perhaps hoping some of the glamour would rub off on him.

Since I loved Park City and didn't have any better offers, I signed a contract and we moved. That summer was idyllic. There was no snow in the area now, just flowers and sunshine. Our condo had a log fireplace, great furniture and was within a stone's throw from the park and the library. A stream ran through the park and the historic town was host to a number of shops and art galleries. We were only 30 minutes from Salt Lake City so Rachelle and the kids could come up and visit often. Money was not a problem for a change and I relaxed.

I visited the old city jail and a church perched high above the town.

I went to the art fair, the theater, the spa. In short, I thoroughly enjoyed myself. The only bad moment came when we discovered Brian's bicycle had been stolen.

I felt like fortune had smiled on me and I had won the jackpot but I kept waiting for the bubble to burst. The songs that had won me the Kentucky Fried Chicken award got me the gig, but it was up to me to keep it.

Music had always come easily to me and I tried. I got up each morning, headed for the local high school auditorium our backer had rented for use as a rehearsal hall. I diligently sat at my piano waiting for something to happen and occasionally we went through a short song list. We did a lot of sitting around. I read magazines. I fidgeted. I played around with chord progressions over my headphones. The drummer or bass guitar player and I made jokes. We went to get snacks. I became distracted. We all started getting anxious.

I'd never had a problem performing in the past, but I was beginning to now, and I wasn't the only one.

The biggest issue was that this man, our producer, backer and boss, didn't know music or musicians.

For three months we practiced daily. We went to work every morning, practicing music. Hi-ho, Hi-ho...It was off to work we go, like Snow White's seven dwarves, although there were twice as many of us at this particular diamond mine.

The problem was that most good musicians don't need that much practice and become bored. They need an audience and stimulation.

Composers generally don't compose on demand. Creativity doesn't punch a time clock. We were all bored and frustrated, and I became jaded and sloppy. I was no longer a performer; I was a robot sitting at a piano.

I wasn't writing anything because our practices were rote and they hadn't asked for any original material. Some of us wondered where this thing was going and what had we gotten ourselves into.

By September, I had lost the faith - and interest. With no enthusiasm for the project any more and no desire to play music, at least temporarily, the spark had gone out of my performance and I was ready to leave. I wanted to tell them some imaginative places where they could put their contract but at that point they were ready to let me and several others go as well.

I never did know what happened to the rest of them or to the project itself, but I ran into one of the other players in Nashville years later and asked what had happened out there after I left. He just made a face and shook his head. I never heard of them again so I assume they never reached the international prominence the backer/producer had hoped for. But Brian and I had a great time in Park City all summer.

Chapter 10

A new career and a new boyfriend

Tumble out of bed and stumble to the kitchen;
pour myself a cup of ambition,
and yawn, and stretch, and try to come to life
jump in the shower, and the blood starts pumping;
out on the street, the traffic starts jumping,
with folks like me on the job from nine to five.

- Nine To Five, Dolly Parton

Moving back to Salt Lake City, I eventually joined another band and got a day job at the Salt Lake Clinic, then one of the Intermountain West's largest outpatient, multi-specialty medical facilities. Judy Prince hired me to be a hospitality coordinator, which they envisioned as a combination receptionist-public relations person.

I sat out in the front lobby and distributed apples, directed traffic through the waiting rooms and assisted wheelchair patients. I monitored the elevators, pointed discreetly to rest rooms, arranged magazines and watered plants. I became the lost and found department, complaint department and security.

This was within the first three days.

Judy also asked for my recommendations on what could be changed or done differently to enhance patient and community relations. She had shown me a stack of patient questionnaires, some of which were quite negative. Long waiting times, inconsistency in scheduling and lack of basic common courtesy were cited as having a negative impact on patients and their families.

From my viewpoint in the front lobby, I had seen receptionists ignore people who may or may not have been in the right place and heard employees rudely telling confused and often ill patients "that's not my department." I had noticed the misleading lettering over registration stations and observed the impersonal nature with which people were often treated. Some of the staff seemed downright unfriendly to me. I could only imagine what it must have been like for a patient.

Always a believer in the Golden Rule and applying some gut-level common sense, I took the writing of these recommendations very seriously. Having already done some freelance marketing and public relations work, I had an intuitive grasp of what needed to happen. As I laid out a plan, I felt that at least some of these folks had lost sight of the fact that the medical profession deals in the healing arts, and patients and their families are the lifeblood. I also felt they had no sense of unification or purpose.

My recommendations included, among other things, basic customer service training at every level. To management's credit, they recognized this need as well, and to my surprise they asked me to develop and implement this program immediately for all employees.

Corporate training was a new direction and on the cutting edge of organizations with vision in the 1980s. I figured it was sort of like teaching, something I hadn't thought of in a long while. Agreeing to try it, I was included in administrative meetings where, as a team, we designed the elements of what I began to call "Extra Mile Training." As the point person, I took notes on everything I saw, both good and bad, concerning every aspect of the clinic and reported back weekly.

I asked everyone from the maintenance department to the doctors what they felt needed to be included in the upcoming training. People even began seeking me out, voicing their opinions about how things should be done.

This was a new direction for them as well as for me.

Because I was now so busy, Judy allowed me to hire my friend Sharon, whom I had met through Rachelle. Also from North Dakota, Sharon had a well-grounded sense of Midwestern practicality, and I felt she could handle anything at the front desk. This freed me to focus on developing the new training program.

As I lay awake at night, thinking about what I could do to make this successful, I decided this course needed to be interactive and bring people together in a very personal sense. I wanted to motivate from within and needed to do whatever I could to make it fun and enjoyable. I later learned that these factors come into play in all adult learning.

Remembering how bored I had often been in different classes, I wondered if I could incorporate some of the entertainer in me into these presentations. I didn't intend to play the piano, but some of my improvisational theater class activities kept coming back to me. I wanted participants to be involved in the experience. Could I combine all of these elements into something that could be covered in a short time frame? How could I help the organization become a team? Could I find a way to not only educate, but also motivate people into changing their behavior? This was a chance to prove myself.

I read everything I could about customer service, training and related subjects. Judy provided me with examples of what other facilities were doing and also sent me to my first training seminar. I researched material, equipment and constantly collaborated with staff.

"Extra Mile Training" evolved into a three-part course that would be taught to small groups from mixed departments. As notices and sign-up sheets were first posted around the time clock, I could hear the moans, groans and cynical tones of displeasure at yet another mandatory meeting.

The first sign-ups were slow in coming, and I was nervous.

In the beginning, folks came with a resigned attitude. A few were already glassy-eyed as they took their seats. As we talked about attitude and professionalism and I asked for their comments and stories, they began to feel that perhaps they too, had a small role in all of this.

Ownership was good, I thought to myself.

At the beginning of the second session, there weren't so many grumbles, and I felt I had even made a few friends. By the time we got through with a first impressions activity I had developed, there were hoots, hollers and peals of laughter coming from the boardroom. We were bonding.

By the time the third session sign-ups were posted, people were eagerly anticipating the class.

From the very first few reluctant attendees, the last few sessions saw people crowding into the boardroom with standing room only, including doctors, the only staff excused from attending.

Participants told stories on themselves about forgetting to reschedule a patient, wearing a dirty smock to work and calling people by the wrong name. Helen in the surgery department - her name often shortened to "Hel"- told how she once answered the busy phone with a very professional sounding "Surgery, this is Hel," leaving someone at the other end of the line wondering, I'm sure, if they should get a second opinion elsewhere.

For some it became a pleasant break in the day, for others, a moment to vent and for still others, a social event. Nurses interacted with billing and maintenance. Receptionists redefined their roles. The end result seemed to be an energizing, cohesive experience with a very high success rate according to participant questionnaires and patient surveys. Two years later, after I had already left the clinic, I was told responses were still much more positive overall.

I had a wonderful mentor in Judy and a great first experience as a new trainer, baptized by fire, and now a dedicated convert. Two big lessons I learned were that in this setting, like in show business, enthusiasm counted and it helped to know your audience.

I had a career, loved the clinic and was working with friends and an administrative staff I admired. I was also still taking classes, playing music and acting on the side. But trouble was brewing.

With Desert Storm in 1991, legions of our doctors left. As their units were called out, we rapidly went from a bustling building, thriving with activity to a shell of our former self. At about this same time, our generator was hit by lightning. All of this added up to a necessary reduction in force. As I talked with Judy, I realized that either Sharon or I would have to leave and I volunteered. I had another direction to pursue.

I had dated mostly other musicians and actors because that was who I met socially. It also seemed they sometimes understood the difference between falling in love with a character and the real person. But most of those romances ended quickly because many of them had a propensity toward ego, financial and personal problems.

My most consistent boyfriend for the past several years had been Gino, a talented drummer and vocalist. He was friendly, intelligent and good-looking, with an infectious sense of humor. I grew to love his family as well, and they treated me like a daughter. I even brought him home for Christmas one year, but our extended relationship was hampered by his substance abuse. It became apparent that I was making the same mistakes all over again.

Eventually, we drifted into a platonic friendship and I began dating others, swearing off anyone in show business.

Shortly before moving to Park City, Buzzy, a fellow musician, came over to discuss our next gig, bringing a friend with him who was *not* a musician. I barely noticed the gentleman until he opened his mouth.

"You shore are purty..." he drawled. I was without makeup, a towel around my just-washed hair, in a paint-spattered shirt and torn shorts. But he was serious. And he had an accent.

"Where are you from?" I asked instantly. He sounded like my Dad's relatives.

"East Tennessee," he replied in that unmistakable mountain accent.

"Where in East Tennessee?" I wanted to know.

"Lenoir City, near Knoxville," he replied. "You shore are purty."

Knoxville! The home of friendly mountains and my childhood dreams, my father's people, Baptist churches and grits. (We didn't have grits in Wisconsin *or* Utah at that time, as far as I knew.) I was predisposed to like anyone who talked that way, especially when he said I was "purty."

However, I was still focused on school, work, motherhood and an upcoming show. It was proposed that we visit the club. Buzzy and I rode in the front seat of my two-seat sports car while his friend Lynn arranged himself in a position worthy of a contortionist to fit within the hatchback rear.

While at the club, perched at the nearly deserted bar between Buzzy and Lynn, I asked the bartender if they had milk, always my drink of choice. I was serious, but they jokingly said they didn't, so I pretended to pout, declined to order anything and became engrossed in conversation with Buzzy, on my left, about bookings, amplifiers, vocalists, transportation, songs, practice and more.

Unnoticed, Lynn, to my right, quietly disappeared, walked to a corner convenience store, brought back a small carton of milk, poured it into a wine glass back at the bar and added a straw. When I finally turned around, there was my precious milk and a twinkle in the bluest eyes I had ever seen.

Buzzy and Lynn were Vietnam Veterans. Lynn had come West hoping to find some of the Marines with whom he had served. A former carpenter by trade, he was attending vocational school, getting counseling at the Vietnam Veteran's Outreach Center and trying to start a brand new life. Unmarried and with no children, he even played on the Vet Center softball team. He had been granted a 30 percent disability from the Veteran's Administration based on something called Post-Traumatic Stress Disorder.

I added him to my dating roster, but we didn't see each other exclusively. Still, he fascinated me.

We went to the Military Museum at Fort Douglas on one of our first dates. It was near the Fourth of July and somewhere a series of firecrackers went off. Lynn dove for cover and I laughed, thinking he was doing it to be funny. He wasn't.

He was patient but persistent and always the epitome of a Southern gentleman around me. Gradually, we became closer.

Lynn was very good with children: mine, Rachelle's and every other child with whom he came into contact. He blamed his own childless state on Agent Orange, a defoliant and herbicide used by U.S. forces in Vietnam. He was very bitter about this as well as other aspects of his military service. His intense dislike and mistrust of the VA was public knowledge to all who knew him, and many other Vietnam vets we knew felt the same way. He only half-jokingly said he wanted to marry a woman with a child, or children, so that they could then draw something from the VA after he was gone.

Lynn had a dynamic personality although he was quiet much of the time. He was the type who spoke softly but carried a big stick, reminiscent of Mel Gibson's character in the *Lethal Weapon* films. Appearance wise, they could have been twins in the movie *Braveheart*.

There was no doubt in my mind that this man could stare the devil down and quite likely had already done so. Mere death was no match for Lynn Edward Morgan. He would only go when he was good and ready. This was a man who could withstand the furies of hell, yet would say a prayer over a dead bird and tenderly tuck a small boy's blanket in around him at night. With time, I realized his intensity, determination and good looks outshone any of my previous suitors and soon I was in love. I didn't want to admit it though. I didn't need any romantic entanglements, and this man's future path was a huge question mark.

He had been a leather-clad biker back in Tennessee and still hung, more or less, with a burly bunch of guys, many of whom were also vets. They wore black clothes, chains and boots and some looked as if they'd as soon kill you as look at you, but all were very protective of Brian and me, treating us with the utmost respect and courtesy.

Lynn continually wanted to show me off to his friends, family and anyone else available. If a piano was around, he would insist that everyone listen to me play. Sometimes it was embarrassing, but it was nice that he was so proud. He had a sense of morality and justice that I could relate to, and he was trying to make things better in his own life, also something I could relate to. Uneducated in the formal sense, he had an intellect that grasped ideas quickly and always sought knowledge. He was brave, gallant, generous, kind and handsome.

I couldn't resist his penetrating blue eyes, single-minded determination and soft-spoken Southern accent and in March of 1989 we were married in a hastily thrown together wedding at the Veterans Outreach Center.

Dad made a quick trip from Wisconsin for the ceremony. He and Lynn bonded - I think it was a Southern man thing or maybe it was because they had both served in the military. The office manager had a small wedding cake, and a former Marine Chaplain presided. I could only find one cassette tape in my car on the way to my wedding, thus, I walked down the makeshift isle to the opening strains of Lynyrd Skynyrd's redneck anthem: *Free Bird.*

As man and wife, we both felt an eternal bond, and Lynn took his parenting responsibilities very seriously, probably more seriously than I did.

We had heard from Dave occasionally through the years, but had received little or no financial support. Lynn became as much of a father figure in Brian's young life as anyone ever had, teaching him "manly" things like knife throwing and woodcarving. He made us biscuits and gravy and had a finely developed sense of what was morally right, even if he didn't always adhere to it.

Feeling sorry for our pet goldfish one night, confined to its tiny bowl, he sneaked it into the apartment complex swimming pool. It apparently swam freely, very hard, fast and erratically for several minutes before undoubtedly succumbing to the high chlorine content. I was furious but finally agreed that it probably had one hell of a last ride and went out with a bang. Lynn brought us a tiny kitten to compensate. He still tried to study, attend classes and take odd jobs.

Brian thought of Lynn as a man's man and tried to be like him, eventually even mimicking his facial expressions and mannerisms. I found comfort and warmth in his arms and a spiritual closeness that defied explanation.

That year, for the first time, I didn't travel home to Wisconsin for Christmas. We lived in a house high on the edge of the Wasatch range, overlooking the twinkling lights of Salt Lake City. With my new husband asleep on the couch and my son playing quietly in his room, I felt contented and whole, as a soft snow fell on Christmas Eve. I was at peace.

It was my best holiday ever.

But my husband had deeper problems than I could ever imagine. Lynn was trying to get a 100 percent disability rating during this time, which involved obtaining numerous records and documentation. I was glad to be able to help but it finally took the efforts of then-Senator Al Gore Jr. to slice through the bureaucratic red tape. When Lynn finally did receive his 100 percent status, it was with back pay. He went to the bank, cashed his check in $10s, $20s and $50s, and was literally rolling around on a bed full of money when I came home to help him celebrate.

He had wanted to help support us and had tried through his original meager disability check and assorted odd jobs, but he still wasn't equipped to support a family even with the increase in his monthly income.

It soon became clear that with habits like smoking and eventually, drinking, to support that I would always be the major breadwinner.

Even though I still didn't indulge in either of these activities, surprisingly, I didn't mind that he did. It seemed to help calm him and he tried to help as much as he could.

When I first met Lynn he didn't drink much, but his nerves were shot and he had constant tremors that became worse over time. A counselor told me my husband was shell-shocked from his experiences in Vietnam, only it was now called Post-Traumatic Stress Syndrome. Lynn told me he hadn't been faking the dive for cover at the sound of firecrackers and was startled easily. He had nightmares and suffered from depression.

In the beginning he didn't speak much of Vietnam, but eventually confided that he occasionally had fleeting suicidal thoughts and wondered why he had survived the jungle warfare when so many didn't. Sometimes in his anxiety he would become desperate and get his medications confused or drink too much.

I tried to soothe him and learned all I could about Vietnam. I learned about the history of our country's involvement in the conflict, what the soldiers went through and what PTSD was. Eventually, I learned about the many vets who had taken their own lives and the ones for whom Vietnam still raged on in their minds, their dreams and often in their lives. I learned about the shells of men who fought such a confusing battle with no lines drawn, no enemy figurehead to blame and little support at home.

I didn't feel sorry for Lynn. I respected him and felt he respected me, but also felt an underlying current of desperation in him that increased over the months.

My husband put me on a pedestal. I was a good woman, the little wife, as opposed to what he called "the shady types that men just like to have fun with." And eventually, he did run around. His infidelity hurt when I found out, and I didn't exactly take it lying down, but felt that what we had was of a deeper nature.

When confronted with proof of her husband's liaisons with other women, Coretta Scott King, Martin Luther King's widow, wrote that such matters in a union between soul mates are ultimately inconsequential.

In the end, I felt the same way.

We had arguments and spats like any other couple, but there was never any damage to the foundation of the relationship. His dalliances seemed to mean nothing to him. *We,* on the other hand, were his family, which was altogether different, in his eyes.

Lynn was always very protective of us. When there was an intruder, Lynn went after him with a stick and I felt sorry for the stranger who, very likely, was a confused or drunken neighbor in the wrong apartment.

He was a generous host, inviting friends in and staying up late with louder music than I would have liked. Over time, if he slept, he slept fitfully and woke often. He seemed even more agitated and had a very rough time each year around July 4th.

Increasingly, he would seemingly be seized with a panic and fear that I didn't understand.

Some may find this hard to believe but those who knew Lynn knew that in spite of the substance abuse, womanizing, panic attacks and stress related symptoms, he still had a very spiritual nature. He spoke with my church members and respected all religions. He respected anyone's relationship with God, Mother Earth and their own spirituality and had a particular interest in Native American teachings.

I often felt him capable of anything, in an almost superhero sense. Still part old-fashioned Southern gentleman and part crazed, redneck war hero, if Lynn had been determined to fly, I was quite sure he could have. If someone had double-dog-dared him to catch a live rattlesnake with his bare hands and eat it raw, I was sure he could have done that, too. Or he might have at least tried, in the right mood.

I also felt the intensity of his love and devotion to us, in spite of his wandering eye and increasing dependence on alcohol or pills. However, his blood-soaked nightmares, punctuated with Vietnamese words I couldn't understand, sometimes terrified me, and I didn't always sleep with my troubled husband.

Pictures

My first home - Grandpa & Grandma's house in Albion, WI

Grandpa (Tata) & Grandma McCarthy, Albion, WI, 1953

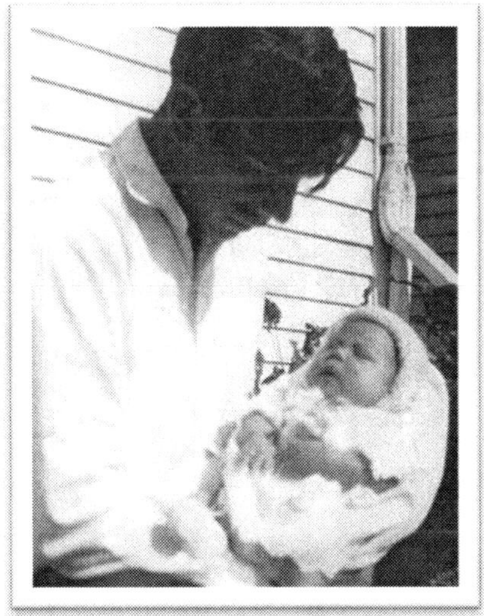

Dad and his infant daughter, 1954

Mom, Dad and their bouncing baby girl, 1955

Mom and a little brother for me. 1957

Carla Jean and Clark, 1957

Future rock 'n roller - Grandma's house 1957

A birthday cake for me, 1958

Papa, Memo, a favorite doll and me in my tutu, 1958

Carla Jean & Clark, 1962

The house in Janesville, 1963

Me and my glasses, 1967

Rebel without a Cause, 1970

Tumbleweed Rock, 1972

Production of 'School for Scandal' set in the 1920's, 1973

From an Avant-garde production of 'Madame De Sade.
I'm the cat on the left. 1974

My cousin Lois, from the 'outlaw' days of country music, 1974

Me at my keyboard, Norfolk, VA, 1976

Publicity photos taken the day I found out I was pregnant, West Virginia 1978

Wedding number 1, Sept 4, 1978

Brian and Mommy, Provo, UT 1981

Head shot, Salt Lake City, 1983

Modeling assignment in Salt Lake City, 1984

Backstage, in costume, Las Vegas, NV, 1985

Brian and friend, Salt Lake City, 1986

My dream car, 1987

University of Utah campus, 1987

On the yacht in San Diego, 1987

Rock Goddess, 1988

The new Mr. and Mrs. Lynn Morgan, March 13 1989

At my piano, Lenoir City, TN, 1992

With Jo Ann, at Mom and Dad's house, Janesville, WI, 1993

Blondie, 1994

The Roselady, 1996

House on Highland Ave., Knoxville, 1997

Celebrating with my keyboard, 1999

I told you my college education would pay off! Nashville, 2002

With Nashville columnist 'Ms. Cheap,' a.k.a. Mary Hance and some of my UAW-Ford family, 2003

Me and Johnny's horses, 2004

Sharon, Rachelle, me and Rachelle's Mom on a cruise, 2005

Me as Charlie Chaplin, 2006

Performing with Rik Roberts as Barney Fife, Memphis, 2006

Performing with 'Zebediah P. Crosscreek' a.k.a. Doug Turpin, Pigeon Forge, TN, 2007

Performing with Patty Waszak, Pigeon Forge, TN, 2008

C.J. As Dolly Parton with some happy fans, 2009

Part 3
Tennessee

Chapter 11

Another relocation, Requiem

No place to run to
Where I did not feel that war
When I got home I stayed alone
And checked behind each door
Cuz I'm still in Saigon
Still in Saigon
I am still in Saigon
In my mind

- *Still in Saigon, Charlie Daniels*

Various stays in VA hospitals and medication didn't seem to do Lynn any good, so we wondered if moving back home to Tennessee would help. We had to do something, and I had always loved it there anyway. Married for just a year, he went on ahead, staying at his mother's while I wrapped things up in Salt Lake City and prepared to move.

We spoke daily for those months we were apart, calling toll-free from the Veteran's Outreach Center where we had wed. We wrote letters and sent pictures in addition to the daily phone calls.

In the spring, he wrote *"All the happiness I will ever have lies with you and Brian."* But he also wrote *"The dreams follow me and I never rest…."*

One of his letters reads:

Dear Carla,

I don't know what to say nor how to say it. After you called I tried to think…it seems impossible. You do not deserve to be treated badly and I'm sorry. Seems everyone knows what's best for me except me. Everyone reads things into me that just aren't there. All I see before me is death in the end and hopefully peace thereafter. I pray for release but wake up alive and depressed daily.

I am no coward but think if I release myself from this life it would be the cruelest thing I have done by far. Not for me but others and I've hurt others enough.

You are a good wife and I don't deserve you. I'm trapped behind bars that don't exist. Time only lets me know what I've always known. It gets worse. I'm so very sorry that I can't be what people expect me to be. Before God, if I could be, I would.

I don't have any answers. Don't even know the questions any more. All I can tell you is, I will keep trying if only I can find a way to find a way.

Please forgive me for the pain I've caused and maybe there will be a way. When and if I can find whatever it is I need, my word will still be good. It's the only thing I haven't lost. They are hollow words, such as my soul but I care all that is possible for you both.

Lynn

P.S. I hope that I was wrong by reading pain in his eyes. Make him understand that I love him.

I'm afraid he did read pain in Brian's eyes. The instability and confusion was getting to both of us.

I'd had letters before, speaking of his depression and always of his love for us, but this was the first time he hadn't signed off with our customary endearment, the Marine Corps motto, Semper Fi. Always Faithful.

This was something he always took very seriously. It had become sort of a code for us, meaning more or less that everything would be all right and our hearts were loyal.

❧

While preparing to join my disturbed husband in Tennessee, I had given notice at the clinic, but was still touring with bands and taking acting jobs whenever possible, knowing money would be tight.

Just before the move, Brian and I were returning from a show in Nevada. Coming across the Bonneville Salt flats at twilight, we stopped at a rest area. As we stepped out of the car, the salt looked almost like snow, and as we stood there with other tourists, a soft, warm wind at our backs, the entire area seemed to take on an ultra-violet glow.

Enveloped in this otherworldly atmosphere with the rugged and barren terrain surrounding us, I felt like I was on another planet with a different colored sun. One of the men in another party explained that this phenomenon was caused by something having to do with the sun's rays reflecting off the salt crystals, but I was too awed to care what caused it.

Once I got over feeling that I was living a *Star Trek* adventure, I simply stood apart from the others and absorbed the feeling of pure energy that washed over me.

It was a spiritual energy, calm and quiet but with a force so powerful it left me speechless. I don't know if others felt it or not, but for me it served as both a warning of tough times ahead and as a well of strength, reinforcement for whatever was to come. I didn't know then how badly I would need the reserve that these few incredible moments had given me

❧

Dad and Mom helped us make the hellish cross-country move. We drove to our new home in Tennessee through Colorado blizzards in the dark, at ridiculous elevations, in two vehicles with Dad pulling a trailer. We had car trouble, got lost and became separated from each other. We finally arrived in Lenoir City, worn out from the trip. Unfortunately, Lynn had not yet found us a place to live. And if anything, his condition had deteriorated.

Mom, Dad, Brian, our two cats and I holed up in a motel as I desperately scrambled to find living quarters. This was difficult because I had no job yet. Dad was getting impatient, and we all felt one of his bad moods coming on. He finally bought us an inexpensive mobile home, had it delivered, unloaded our belongings and left.

Lynn was still staying with his mother and I had the feeling that we had grown apart, but there was still a bond of responsibility and undeniable love between us. We just had different lifestyles. I soon found his to be so convoluted that I almost didn't want any part of it. Erratic and unstable, he at times now seemed a different person than the man I married.

Prior to our Tennessee relocation, I had sent resumes, made telephone contacts and was now hired as a part-time instructor with a business college in Knoxville. I taught English, leadership, human relations and more. Later promoted to full-time placement director, I had phenomenal success primarily because my predecessor had done very little.

I updated records, implemented job hunting workshops, support systems and an externship program. I enjoyed the work and even enjoyed the 30-minute commute each day.

I also began playing with a band in a small club in my father's old stomping ground, Union County. Some of the patrons knew my aunts, uncles and other relatives from way back, and I felt warm and accepted. One of my favorite aunts, long deceased, had been a teacher in an old country school, and I even met people whom she had taught many years ago.

Lynn tried to take occasional carpentry and handyman jobs here and there, but the quality of his work was not up to his own standards and he became increasingly frustrated.

As the VA tried different medications, he lost weight, slept very little, increased his alcohol and pill consumption and eventually became unable to function sexually, though sex had never been the focus of our relationship. At least this put a temporary end to other women, but the substance abuse seemed to get worse along with what I began to call his stress episodes.

When this happened, I could see a change in his face and a different look in his eyes. He would become agitated and have episodes of tears and rage, but never directed at us.

He tried controlling these feelings with more drugs, alcohol, loud music and parties. Eventually this behavior was almost nonstop. I found it increasingly difficult to be around him during these periods, but then he got so that he didn't really want to be around people. He would go off to friends' homes or out in the woods for days on end. One time he told me he was going to go rabbit hunting someday and not come back... except he didn't hunt rabbits or anything else.

I was worried. He was out of control and around people who used some very serious drugs. His behavior was so erratic that despite his reassurances, I felt anxiety each time I saw or talked to him. We had fights and his family, of course, had to choose sides. I was the odd one out. But then we'd make up and be friends. In spite of everything, I still felt loved by my troubled spouse and cared deeply for him.

He acquired a gun and began to keep it with him constantly. He insisted that I learn to use it, taking me to a secluded spot to show me how, but I had never been around weapons of any kind and never got over my fear of the cold, hard metal.

Depression seemed to overcome him at times. He was increasingly wild, but then would calm down and come back to us, apologizing for his behavior. He still stayed at his mother's for the most part. Other times, I wouldn't know where he was, but he would always surface to gently reassure me.

I understood now that Lynn was still seeing other women, not necessarily for sex but for the mutual shared exhilaration of drugs. He took risks of all kinds and seemed to invite trouble. The lifestyle was taking its toll on his health. The man was careening down a one-way path of destruction, but in his more lucid moments I could see the terrors of war, wasted years, heartbreak and hopelessness in his eyes along with an unyielding, spiritual love for Brian and me that was miraculously still intact.

Lynn kept telling me that anything he did would be for us, but I had no idea what he was talking about. I felt that way a lot those days.

He considered Brian to be his son and was concerned that he wasn't much of a father. It bothered him that he had nothing to give Brian or leave us upon his death as far as material possessions. He often said we deserved better.

My desperate husband became preoccupied with Desert Storm, which frustrated him because he wanted to re-enlist and knew they wouldn't take him. He tried on his military uniform several times, telling me that he wanted to be buried in it. He even insisted that I take a picture of him while in his uniform.

He once explained that living with the intensity of jungle warfare day after day in Vietnam had become his reality so much that when he returned home it didn't even feel like he was alive any more.

Lynn wasn't the jealous type and didn't blame me for occasionally talking to an old boyfriend from Utah on the phone or going out to lunch sometimes with friends. We both were still in love with each other, but Lynn's demons were winning the battle, and I was trying to break free. He was becoming more like a wayward relative.

It grew more and more difficult to be around him, and I began to see the futility of our relationship. When we were together for any length of time, it felt like being sucked into a whirlpool of anxiety and stress. I was better off being totally away from him.

We amicably discussed divorce on more than one occasion. Lynn said he wouldn't blame me for getting one. He said he wanted whatever I wanted. Eventually I tracked down an inexpensive, no-fault attorney and hesitantly had papers drawn up. When I gave them to Lynn to sign, he took them and quietly said that nothing – not even death – would destroy the bond between us, but he never signed them.

Even during this period, he would come over and try to help out around the house, take us out to eat, visit with Brian and reassure me of his love.

One night, sitting on the porch, he pointed to the brightest star in the sky and playfully said that was my star. He said he named it after me and when he was gone, I should look up into the sky and remember how much he loved me. I giggled at the sentiment, but he didn't.

We discussed trying one more time to make things work. He moved his belongings back in with me, but within days he had begun to project that restless, indefinable anxiety that made me feel on edge and we had a spat on the Fourth of July, 1991.

Brian was visiting in Wisconsin. Lynn and his friends had been drinking more and more throughout the day. Even though I knew he was self-medicating, trying to maintain some control over his shaky mental state and thin body, the drinking and partying always got out of control. If he drank or took enough pills to calm his unsteady nerves, it also slurred his speech, impaired his judgment and changed his personality. Like many others, he and his friends all thought themselves to be 10 feet tall and bulletproof after enough alcohol.

He had never laid a hand on me, but I knew where this was going. I didn't want my home to become a party palace again. I wasn't happy about it and let him know. He glared at me, then left with his friends. They came back in a matter of minutes. They had forgotten the beer.

I knew at that point it was over. I knew I couldn't live like that again. I couldn't take any more. He disappeared only to reappear the next day, quiet and downcast, but sober. We were still civil, friends even, but there was now an air of finality in our relationship. I was, however, very concerned about him as he left.

Later when I took his belongings back over to his mother's house, I began looking for him. I wanted to tell him that I had dropped off his things, that I had paid some money toward an old classic car he was hoping to have restored and that I still loved him, no matter what, even though we couldn't be together.

I had a sick feeling in the pit of my stomach and for some reason felt it was imperative that I find him. I had begun to develop a sixth sense about when and where Lynn would appear and could almost feel when he was doing something he shouldn't, much like a mother's intuition. I looked everywhere I knew: at all of his friends and relatives - I even drove up and down certain country roads hoping to find a sign of him. I felt pressured and desperate to find him but still had to go to my job playing music in Union County that night.

Eventually, I had to tear myself away from the search, sick at heart. That night while performing, I was able to put aside my anxieties somewhat, although it felt like I had left something undone.

Lynn was never far from my mind or my heart, but now he felt more like a brother or father figure. He had, in some strange way, become my rock, my mentor and my anchor of stability even though he was not very stable himself. Even when he was not around, he was a presence in my life.

July 6th, 1991. When the night was over and the music played, I accepted a ride back to my car with a young man, an acquaintance with whom I had often visited at the club in Union County.

After reaching my car, I drove the rest of the way home with very mixed emotions and a strange, unusual apprehension, my mind still focused on Lynn. I felt like I was holding my breath.

Arriving home in the wee hours of the morning I found a terse, scribbled note on my door that read "CARLA, CALL RIGHT AWAY – TOOTS." The scrawled capital letters denoted urgency. Toots was Lynn's older sister, with whom I had stayed when I first came to meet his family. As I looked at the note, a rising panic began to grip me. Alone, I began to shake uncontrollably. Time seemed to stand still.

From out of the blue, the quiet, unmistakable voice of a sixth sense whispered that Lynn was gone. I didn't know how or when, I only knew that he was gone forever. He was dead. And I knew without being told that it was by his own hand.

Desperately hoping I was wrong, silently and with still shaking fingers, I dialed, dropping the phone twice. As Toots confirmed my worst fears over the phone, I shouted, "NO...No...no..." and dropped the receiver again. All the stress, emotion, drama, uncertainty and events of the last few years came to a head as I sobbed and screamed uncontrollably. The room spun in slow motion as I gripped the counter, then fell to the floor.

I couldn't live with the man, but didn't know if I could live without him completely. Regret about not finding him earlier was a heavy weight when I finally heard the rest of her words over the phone.

Lynn and his brother had gone to a friend's house. He went into a back bedroom, lay down on a bed, stuck a gun in his mouth and, angling it upward, pulled the trigger.

They had taken him directly to the funeral home and I spent the rest of the sleepless night at Toots' house. The entire family was in shock.

I don't remember much about making funeral arrangements. I know that as I took my first look at his body, lying in his dress blues in the casket, my knees gave out, the room went black and I only remember waking up in a friend's van in the parking lot.

I went back and in the quiet of the funeral home, touched his hand, which was cold beneath the white glove. His lips, the lips I knew so well, seemed ready for a kiss, so I kissed him gently, not wanting to wake him. Only now, strangely, it didn't seem like he was asleep.

Others slept at night. Lynn's sleep, in life, had become so rife with violence, raging nightmares and visions of long ago memories that when asleep, he didn't rest. His nights had become as tortured as the jungle where he had once fought, and his days had become no better. He had, in fact, learned to sleep with his eyes open, when and if he slept at all. His face, in the relatively short time I had known him, had assumed a haggard, haunted look that was now gone. Now, there were no lines in his handsome face, and he looked very much like the picture I had of him at 17 as a young Marine.

In death, he finally slept.

Holding his lifeless body, I whispered that I still loved him. "It's over now, baby, everything's *OK*, it's all right..." I repeated through a torrent of tears.

Long ago on the piano, I had played a medley consisting of *Dixie*, *the Battle Hymn of the Republic,* and the *Marine Corps Hymn* for Lynn. It sounded like Elvis' trilogy, but he thought I had put it together expressly for him and it was his favorite selection. This is what he requested I play when showing me off, and on several occasions he made me promise that I would play this piece at his funeral. I laughingly promised because although death is inevitable, we are seldom prepared for the reality. Denial is the first line of defense.

Mom and Dad came down for the funeral, bringing Brian. My normally stoic father had tears in his eyes.

Brian's shoulders shook, wracked with sobs as he entered the funeral home. He felt guilty that he wasn't there when it happened. Lynn called him the day before, probably to say goodbye, but Brian thinks that if he'd been there, he could have done something to prevent it. The survivor guilt Lynn had felt was now passed on to Brian.

With the help of Valium, I was able to play Lynn's last request and make it through the following days, but I was empty. The day he died, I quit my job. All I wanted to do was sleep and hold him one more time. "If only I'd done this or that..." played over and over in my mind.

Our society has long observed traditional, solemn, ritualized funeral ceremonies as a way of remembering and mourning those who have passed on, with special honors bestowed upon those who served in the armed forces. Honor guards perform these duties at the graveside of the deceased with salutes, flag-draped coffins and the playing of *Taps*.

Usually made up of military retirees and active duty personnel, they are sometimes short the number required for the occasion, whereupon someone else may serve.

Months earlier, I helped Lynn with an honor guard at a funeral where they were short one person. They outfitted me with a uniform and I held a flag as *Taps* was played. It seemed to mean a great deal to Lynn and he told everyone that I made a good little soldier. Now, as that lonely refrain played and they presented me with the folded flag and Brian with Lynn's many medals, I couldn't stop crying.

The next week after the funeral, I went to play music with the band, now my only income. I was still sort of numb, but did all right until, without thinking, the band began a classic country tune called *He stopped Loving Her Today* about a man's death putting an end to his love.

I ran off the stage in tears and out the side door.

Damn you, George Jones.

The night after Lynn's death was the first time I had ever missed a gig. This was the first time I had ever lost my professional composure on stage. I was a basket case. Angry, then sad, then angry again, I didn't know what to be or how I felt about anything.

❧

Somebody had sent flowers and plants from the funeral home to our house immediately following the interment. A week later, I came home to find a note from Blondie, one of Lynn's younger sisters saying "These are for Lynn, *not you*!" Brian said she had seemed angry.

I felt as if the family blamed me for Lynn's death and I wondered about that myself. If I hadn't married him, if we hadn't moved to Tennessee, if I'd insisted on more hospitalization...."What could I have done differently?" was a constant question in my mind.

Blondie wouldn't speak to me, but Toots and the rest of the family were always kind, at least to my face.

I went through the motions of life, filling out VA papers and didn't even know if they would help pay for the cost of the funeral. As I spoke with VA representatives over the phone, at one point I was told that I would be eligible for Lynn's Social Security, too.

"Too? What do you mean too?" I asked the man.

"Well, as a military widow, you are entitled to something called Death and Indemnity Compensation benefits as well as Social Security - he was 100 percent disabled due to a service-connected condition. Those are the magic words right there," he replied.

I was well aware of VA rules and regulations, but they continued to frustrate me. Lynn knew more about them than I did. I knew that DIC benefits were granted to war widows, but Lynn didn't die at war. He died in the barren, back bedroom of a old house with worn, wooden floors.

I knew, I had gone to see the place. The neighbors had told me about burning the mattress he died on.

"My husband shot himself," I flatly told the Veteran's Administration representative over the phone.

"Your husband is dead because of his service-connected condition, Post- Traumatic Stress Disorder. How else could he die from a psychological illness?" he replied.

With that, it dawned on me. Lynn had this planned all along. If he died from his service-connected disability, he would have been able to leave Brian and me with something. And how else *does* one die from a psychological illness?

In recent months, Lynn suspected that he had lymph cancer, one of the carcinomas more common with exposure to Agent Orange. But he would never go see a doctor, to my frustration. If he had died from that, we would not have been eligible for any VA survivors' benefits because that was not his service-connected disability. Even if he had been diagnosed with cancer, then took his own life, the argument could have been made that the suicide was because of a terminal illness, not because of Post-Traumatic Stress Disorder.

All the references to his eventual demise, all the veiled warnings and risk taking, all the paperwork, the VA visits and documentation, his concern about providing for us - added up.

I'd often had the feeling that he was doing his best to drive me away, for my own good, yet at the same time, still loved and was committed to us.

The timing, the method, the detail, even the place was designed to provide as much as possible for Brian and me while allowing for the least trauma.

As long as I don't remarry, I am eligible for certain military benefits. But the suicide of a loved one or family member is always devastating. And I will forever be haunted by a sound I never heard: the gunshot that took Lance Corporal Lynn Edward Morgan's life.

Chapter 12

Tornado

I know your life on earth was troubled
And only you could know the pain
You weren't afraid to face the devil
You were no stranger to the rain.

- Go Rest High on that Mountain, Vince Gill

Willie Ruth and her daughter Diana, my friends from childhood, came to visit before the funeral.

After the funeral, I gave the ceremoniously folded American flag that had draped the casket to Lynn's elderly mother who was too ill to attend.

Our benefits included a small monthly allotment, eligibility for a VA home loan, educational benefits, medical insurance and more, but it couldn't make up for all that had happened. I had never hated Lynn or wished him dead. In retrospect, there were times when I think he was trying to make me hate him. Maybe then I would have been glad about this. But I wasn't.

Incredibly lonely and confused, I began to hate Lenoir City and withdrew from society. With just enough of an income to live on and minimal expenses, I was able to stay at home and sleep for days on end. The days blended into weeks, then months. I went to the grocery store and that was all. I couldn't deal with my own depression, much less the problems Brian was beginning to have.

I would go visit the mausoleum by the lake both day and night, where Lynn lay next to his father. I talked to him like he was there. Frustrated and often angry, sometimes I kicked the marble next to his name. Other times I took a flower. Mostly, I cried.

For months, I was short-tempered and irritable. I felt as though I had no emotions at times, and other times I felt like I had too many. I lacked focus, was on edge and felt like I was the one who had a stress disorder.

Mom finally came to visit us from Wisconsin, and we argued. It became a yelling match, escalating to a point where I was practically screaming. I don't even remember the cause of the disagreement, but in the immediate aftermath of my world-class rant she quietly pointed out that it was the one-year anniversary of Lynn's death and I needed to get a grip.

Instead of yelling back, I realized she was right. That night, it had been exactly one year since that awful phone call, since I'd collapsed on the floor, hysterical. Since I'd lost it. And I was about to do it again. Instead, about midnight, I quietly went alone again to the mausoleum.

This time, I was calm and accepting and just prayed. In the quiet stillness of the night, the street light next to the building slowly faded to dark, then came back on again slowly as I watched. This happened three times as I stared, transfixed, looking out the window. It had never happened before when I visited. For some reason, it seemed to have a slight comforting effect on me, like it was some sort of sign.

In the coming years, people witnessed weird and unexplained electrical activity present wherever Brian or I went. My practical nature dismisses anything illogical or not immediately explainable, but a psychic friend later told me that my husband's energy was very close to me, causing the phenomenon. Whether one believes in such things or not, I found it strangely comforting. It was time to try and put the pieces of my life back together.

I began seeing a psychiatrist, contacted the University of Tennessee about graduate school, put a "For Sale" sign on our home and started looking for a job. Miraculously, a job came looking for me.

One of the contacts I had made before leaving Utah was with the Job Training Partnership Act in East Tennessee, part of a national program designed to promote employment among the disadvantaged.

As a single parent living below poverty level in Utah, this agency helped me become self-sufficient, even getting me appropriate clothing to wear to job interviews and bus fare on occasion.

I knew that as my friends and I tried to better ourselves by getting an education, often it wasn't the obvious reasons that held us back.

Financial aid was available for tuition, and studying was often not the problem. Sometimes it was transportation, finances, childcare, self-esteem, appearance, health problems, grooming, lack of social skills or any number of other factors.

I remembered my friend Penny who packed up and left school mid-quarter, overwhelmed by stress. I knew firsthand what it was like to struggle with these issues and as I overcame obstacles I was motivated to do more for others in that situation.

While still in Salt Lake City, I developed a program addressing some of these concerns. It seemed to help those who participated, and I hoped I could do the same elsewhere.

Now, one of the directors of this agency in Loudon County contacted me and asked if I would be interested in helping to develop a work training program in an underutilized facility about 20 miles from Lenoir City. Technically, it was under the jurisdiction of a certain local college, but it was in such an outlying area that it could be used to serve several counties and other schools.

Would I? I jumped at the chance.

They sent me to Tellico West Industrial Park where a state-of-the-art learning facility sat quietly on the shores of the lake, surrounded by manufacturing companies. I could use my discretion, imagination and every resource available to build a program to help disadvantaged and unemployed participants. This was to be a collaborative effort of more than a dozen agencies and organizations.

The first thing I did was contact the area employers.

As I went from one meeting to another, I made friends with the human resource departments. I asked what they were looking for in employees. I asked them to describe their ideal worker. What were their job requirements? What was their single biggest complaint? What direction was their company headed in the future?

In the early '90s, almost all organizations were looking into management and operating methods pioneered by W. Edwards Deming and were incorporating some form of Total Quality Management into their procedures. I resolved to learn all I could about this new process. In June of 1992, as a new member of the American Society for Training & Development, I was one of a group randomly selected to attend Total Quality Awareness Training at nearby McGhee-Tyson Air Base, the first time civilians were offered this week long military course. Through this experience, I learned about teambuilding, problem solving and the role of continuous improvement in quality.

From my visits with industry, I learned firsthand about transformative processes in a manufacturing environment and change in organizational culture. I learned how difficult it often was to become a cooperative, functioning team. I learned to read a statistical process control chart. I came to understand how important training and motivation were to the overall success of any project. I learned how technology and computerization were being incorporated into every process. And I learned that personal responsibility was all-important.

A plant was closing its doors near Athens, Tenn. Some 300 workers were going to be losing their jobs and needed help finding new ones.

This became my first assignment.

We scheduled three weeks of daily classes for two large groups. As my students came in that first day, I could see the resignation and bitterness on their faces. I could tell some felt like giving up. Perhaps the best thing I could give them was hope, I thought to myself.

Again, like in Salt Lake City, I wanted to involve them and make them a part of the class, not just preach or lecture to them. With my outline of subjects and all the things we needed to cover, perhaps none was more important than the items on my personal development list.

These included many of the subjects from the programs I'd developed previously, from self-esteem to grooming.

Losing a job is always a devastating experience, especially if one has a family to feed and bills to pay which everyone did. Many had to get beyond their anger in order to deal with the reality of the situation, so, again, class became a place to vent. Eventually though, we moved on to more positive thinking, setting goals and filling out applications. I brought in speakers, and we visited the area industries. Eventually I heard that many of these folks found new jobs.

They were a wonderful bunch of people who just needed some help adjusting and probably would have found jobs with or without the program. However, because this program was considered a success, I was asked to take on a new assignment. My goal this time: to help high school dropouts between the ages of 17 and 21 obtain their General Education Diplomas or GEDs, job training and work skills.

High school dropouts were right up my alley! I revisited my high school years and remembered all I'd hated about them. My superiors were open to any suggestions I had, but they wanted to make it into a work-study program.

With buy-in from the many different agencies and organizations, it became a project worthy of press attention, which I utilized to help recruit students. Once again, my public relations background came in handy. By the time the program was ready to start, we had about 30 young people with varying degrees of motivation and commitment.

Instead of concentrating on academics and taking a hard line approach, I went out of my way to make learning fun and incorporated team-building activities. We went on field trips, had speakers and played games.

We had volunteers and friends in state agencies. Peer pressure was directed toward attending classes and developing support for each other instead of competition. Activities were designed to encourage initiative, enhance problem-solving skills and focus on the student as a whole.

I now had state vans for transportation, a paid staff of six and several volunteers. My role was similar to that of a school principal as well as instructor, but I was more like a friend to staff as well as students. I simply didn't believe the dogmatic, authoritarian approach would work with this group so I did anything I could to stay away from it. Instead, I encouraged personal responsibility and creative, unusual approaches to motivation and learning.

Some of my students had never been outside of their county. As I expanded their horizons by taking them places, they expanded my knowledge of their lives.

Late one night, I was dropping several of them off individually after a big day at the county fair in Knoxville. When I came to one young lady's family home, back so far in the country I feared never finding my way out again, she seemed nervous and in a hurry. As she opened the van door to the black night, a curious, strong odor enveloped the vehicle. Thinking it smelled like antifreeze, I groaned aloud and wondered if the van were going to give us engine trouble. It certainly smelled like it might overheat.

"Don't you know the smell of mash?" asked a sleepy student incredulously from the rear.

Mash was a component involved in the making of homemade corn liquor - moonshine.

I tried to teach my students to think for themselves and to develop opinions based on sound logic and reason. I would ask them what they thought about things and why they thought that way.

One young lady was dumbfounded. She looked perplexed as she asked, "You want to know what I think?...Me?... All by myself?" I nodded and listened.

"Well...er..." she looked at the floor, then tried again. "I, ummm... what do I think...ahh...I, uh..."

Clearly she was having trouble with this concept. Either that or she was having trouble making up her mind. Not wanting to pressure anyone, I gently turned to the next person in our little group.

The first young lady approached me after class.

"Miss Morgan, nobody's ever wanted *my* opinion before. Nobody's ever cared what I thought about anything. First my daddy told me what to do and what to think, then my husband did.... I don't think I've ever thought for myself before."

Three days later she came and told me what she thought about a LOT of things. She seemed excited that somebody cared enough to listen.

A couple of my instructors worked with students individually on academics, but it was amazing how much these young people could do on their own once motivated and with a little support. One by one, as I took them to take the GED test, they passed, sometimes much to their own amazement.

Success builds upon success, and I was very proud of our students.

A young man and woman who met in class came to me for counseling, saying they wanted to get married. They seemed to think I would be angry or disapprove. Instead, I asked them how they felt about each other.

I asked about her small child from a previous relationship who would be affected by the union and asked them about their plans for the realities of life, reminding them that they were adults. Then I asked them to consider, when they had trouble as all couples do, how they would feel looking at the other lying in a casket, where they would never be able to kiss or touch or hold the other again and to ask themselves if the trouble was really worth it. I remembered all too well.

Four years later I heard they were still happily married, gainfully employed and had another child on the way.

The success of this new program could not be ignored, and it all but forced the affiliated college to do more with the facility. I had been told that if these projects were successful, then I would most likely be made director of what would ultimately become a premier job training/vocational facility.

We were now serving two different geographical units of the same agency, two separate colleges and three counties. Responsibility was transitioning from the incumbent organization to the one that should have been in charge in the first place. We were completing two sets of paperwork on each student, and my staff and I were working on a month-to-month contract, never knowing who would be paying our salaries from one paycheck to the next. Rules changed from one day to the next, and I was getting frustrated.

Without any notice, they brought in a man from Nashville with ties to the Tennessee Department of Labor, announcing that he would be the director. The man seemed nice enough, but I wondered what, if anything, they planned to do with me. After all my hard work and success, apparently someone else was going to be in charge.

This man had very different ideas about education than I did and began working toward making it an almost military-style facility. He brought in camouflage uniforms and prepackaged military food. I dutifully donned a flight suit, kept doing the unexpected and applied my own philosophy of education wherever possible.

I felt I couldn't, however, guarantee the continued success of this particular program and felt betrayed by those in charge, whoever they now were.

In spite of my disappointment at the turn of events and current overload at work, I was loyal to and proud of my students, so I swallowed hard and scheduled a graduation ceremony at a local restaurant. This meant very much to some of them. Two area banks contributed small scholarships, and Mom and Dad came down to join the festivities.

The new director was there, along with the bank representatives and some of the students' families. It was a turning point for many of them - and for me. The program was ongoing, but the next time they came around with a contract, I declined, ready to move on. I had begun graduate studies at the University of Tennessee and wanted a change.

Before I left my job, Brian and I were spending a calm, leisurely Sunday at home in Lenoir City when the door gently blew open. We both looked at each other, smiled and said the same thing: "Lynn's here," referring to the ghost of the man we both missed. Brian then looked out the front door and said, "Mom, I think it's a tornado!"

I said, "Naw...they don't have tornadoes in Tennessee." But it *was* a tornado.

Feb. 21, 1993, we crouched wide-eyed at the window in Brian's room and watched as trash cans, debris and branches blew past our mobile home and hail pelted the earth over the next 10 or 15 minutes. Rivers of rain and gusts of wind carried clothes, lawn furniture and toys down the hill.

Mom had been in a terrible tornado in Oklahoma as a child. Growing up in Wisconsin, I often stood out on the front porch during tornado warnings and watches. Several towns nearby had been hit hard. Dad and some of his fellow workers had even gone to help clean up the town of Monroe, Wis., but I had never actually been in one.

When the worst of it appeared to be over, we got in our car but couldn't get very far. Trees blocked the roads and traffic was at a standstill. Flashing lights and sirens were everywhere, and the sky had that sickly yellow look of death through the rain that was still falling. Listening to the radio reports, it sounded like half of Lenoir City had been destroyed. We could see pieces of buildings, trash and flash floods everywhere. Lynn had taught me what to do in a crisis: stay calm, think quickly, take action and help wherever possible.

Help wherever possible? I couldn't get anywhere in my car to help anyone because by now Lenoir City was off limits to travelers of any kind, like a war zone.

I came home, dropped Brian off and changed clothes and vehicles. I loaded up the state van with the military food - MRE's (Meals Ready to Eat) that were stashed at my house. The students didn't like them anyway. The National Guard was already on the scene. With my official van and flight suit, I'm sure everyone thought I was one of them.

I drove as far as I could, then got out and walked. The damage was unbelievable and devastating. The laundromat near our home was completely gone. Trees were toppled, destroying cars and homes. Businesses were in shambles. It had barely missed us. Bringing the food and blankets I had hastily thrown into the van to a church hall that was a temporary shelter, I then went to help clean up, pushing branches and debris out of the roadway.

Coming back to the hall, I helped console a woman and two children, who appeared to be in shock. Another woman was shivering so I wrapped her in a blanket. A block away, an older woman was trapped inside her home where rescuers were trying to free her.

The first aid kit in the van came in handy as I washed a couple of minor cuts on a teenager near an area where part of a house had been destroyed.

I gave rides to those who had no transportation as far as I could travel through the blocked roads. As it grew dark, I watched the rescue efforts and handed out food to hungry Guard members. Later, I delivered more military meals and other items to workers and helped clean up into the night.

Exhausted, I returned home to tell Brian what was going on and fell into a deep sleep, still wearing my combat boots.

Chapter 13

The TV set incident

You better stop, look around
Here it comes, here it comes, here it comes, here it comes
Here comes your 19th nervous breakdown.

- 19th Nervous Breakdown, The Rolling Stones

In January of 1993, through a quirk of fate, I was able to attend the inauguration of President William Jefferson Clinton and Vice President Al Gore. This was the first time I had ever visited Washington D.C. and in spite of the cold, it was exciting, abuzz with talk of the new administration and crowded with visitors.

I saw landmarks that I had previously seen only in pictures, movies or on television like the Washington Monument and the White House, and I was caught up in the bustle of the city. The sense of history was not lost on me and I felt very patriotic, standing on the steps of our nation's capitol. I saw Aretha Franklin, Jimmy Buffet, Bob Dylan, the Dixie Chicks (pre-Natalie Maines) and other performers during the few days I was there. The Clinton inaugural and balls were definitely a nod to the younger generation and had the celebratory feel of a huge party. Although I had spent time in large metropolitan areas before, I walked around like a hick who had just fallen off the turnip truck, trying to take everything in.

On my last night there, after leaving the evening's event, I took a taxi to the one place I had not gone yet and wasn't even sure I wanted to go. Stepping out onto the wet pavement, I took a deep breath and walked a short stretch to the only place my late husband wanted to visit but never had. His death had affected me profoundly and although I'd begun to move on, I still grieved and hadn't experienced closure of any kind.

As I tentatively touched the cold black granite of the Vietnam Veterans Memorial, I was touched by the sheer number of human emotions this monument represented. The pain and suffering of the soldiers and their families, the confusion and havoc wrought in our country during the years of the Vietnam conflict and the horrors of war in general came together here. It seemed that I could feel a spirit of sacrifice.

As I slowly walked the length of this stone shrine under the streetlights, I was unable to look away. I remembered the grainy black and white footage on TV of a far-off place called Vietnam that I watched as a child. I thought of the many that I personally knew who had lost loved ones in that strange land. I paused and wondered if any of the names engraved on this massive wall had been my husband's comrades. Had they shared a cigarette somewhere in the jungles of Southeast Asia? Had they hidden near a rice paddy, listened for the sound of helicopters or dodged firefights together?

The sounds of the city were muffled in that sacred place and I said a quiet prayer for all who had been touched by war. At that moment, I knew that Lynn had joined his fallen brothers, where he felt he had belonged for more than twenty years.

It was time for me to let go.

While visiting D.C. had been a turning point of sorts, I had genuinely loved Lynn and was only in Lenoir City because of him. While I hadn't felt that his sister Blondie and I were enemies, she was a woman of extremes, and it had been obvious on her part that there was no love lost toward me. In her grief at Lynn's death, she had looked for a place to lay blame and placed it squarely on my shoulders.

However, we had mutual friends. Some of Lynn's family liked me and I had always been kind to everyone. I never spoke ill of Blondie – or anyone, for that matter. Eventually our mutual friends made an impression on her, she heard good things about me and warily visited several times in the presence of others. Although I had never made overtures or gone out of my way to correct her misguided opinion of me, she finally approached me alone with tears in her eyes and said

"You know, you're not so bad…"

Surprised, I said, "Why, thank you."

"I've heard a lot of good things about you from folks."

"I'm really a good person," I said, lowering my voice and glancing around, secretively.

Looking at the floor, she said, "I've misjudged you terribly. Do you think…Can you ever forgive me?"

Blondie, the sister-in-law who had been my greatest antagonist had now become my greatest supporter. We became the best of friends.

She, like Lynn, had a bit of a wild streak, and out of the entire family, I thought her to be the most like him. With a cigarette attached to her lower lip, she was very direct and could cuss like a sailor but also like her late brother, she had a heart of gold.

In the midst of a divorce, she and her small son eventually came to live with Brian and me temporarily in our mobile home. We had long talks about many things, healed each other's spirits and began to go out with a group of her friends from work. Always the designated driver, I still didn't drink, but I had fun dancing. It felt like I was rejoining the living and finally moving on.

A promise I had made to Lynn was that if anything should ever happen to him, I would try and spend as much VA money as I could. Bitter over the way he and his military brothers had been treated, he even wanted Brian to be able to go to college on his "VA dime" as well.

With this in mind, in the Spring of 1992, while still employed at Tellico, I began working on a master's degree at the University of Tennessee.

I also thought staying very busy would help me deal with my ongoing grief. One of the few programs I could enter quickly was in the field of educational psychology. Adult education was offered as a specialization. It was combined, at that time with human resource development.

This was exactly the field with which I had been involved for months now. I felt like I had been fishing for a while; it was now time to get my fishing license.

Thinking that I had nothing to lose with the VA paying for it, I wasn't overly enthusiastic and was terribly intimidated at the very first class I attended.

Awed by the affable, knowledgeable professor, the class scared me and I didn't go back, thinking I was out of my league. I didn't think I could compete on that playing field. But Professor Brockett eventually became a good friend and mentor and soon I was hooked on grad school.

I had no regrets about the excellent education I received at the University of Utah, but grad school was altogether different. Focusing on one primary area instead of the myriad of extraneous classes like in my undergraduate program, a student could pursue their main interest in depth.

The faculty and staff, as well as my fellow students, were supportive, challenging and nurturing. I became focused on theories of learning, reflective practice and the different types of research. We were encouraged to think creatively. Self-directed learning was expected. Most classes were interactive, and I felt very much a part of campus life even though I was terribly busy with my job, my students and Brian.

In May of 1993, halfway through my master's program, I left my position at Tellico and made plans to move into Knoxville. Looking for a job and a place to live, I was delighted when Blondie called asking if I wanted to go out that evening. Little did I know the impact my casual reply would have on my future.

This would be the night friends and family members later refer to as "the infamous TV set incident." Halfway through the evening at a lavish dining and dancing establishment, a wall-mounted device holding a television set in place malfunctioned, causing it to fall on me as I sat at the table. No one knows how or why it fell, but the fact that it did would change my life forever.

After leaving the emergency room that night, I staggered in and told my son, then age 13, what happened. He thought, for a moment that I was "drunk" and told me later that he was shocked by my appearance and behavior.

I then slept for almost 24 hours.

The following week I contacted an attorney, already knowing that I was going to have ambulance and emergency room bills. He was not a personal injury lawyer but a friend. At his office on Monday, I was still dazed, confused, sleepy and a bit dizzy, which I attributed to lifelong inner ear problems.

He put me in his car and personally drove me to see a neurologist who, in turn, admitted me to a local hospital for further testing. I wasn't told the results of those tests but was released after a couple of days and went back home, intending to resume life and school as usual. I was honored to have just been awarded a $1,000 scholarship from the American Business Women's Association to finish my graduate studies and was even thinking of pursuing doctoral-level work.

I had already put myself through school at the University of Utah as a single parent, had earned several impressive letters of recommendation from progressively responsible jobs, had just bought my very first brand-new car and was beginning to enjoy the single life again. I was also playing music almost every weekend with a local band and beginning to come out of my self-imposed shell.

Within a week of this freak accident, however, I could barely shift gears while driving, the two middle fingers on my right hand didn't seem to function, I suffered intense jaw pain, and couldn't move my head from side to side. I was still slightly dizzy, and it seemed like I had a constant headache. The pain was so intense at times that I found myself willing to take any drug available to alleviate it, something totally out of character for an outspoken anti-drug, anti-alcohol crusader.

Not knowing where else to turn, my attorney sent me to a chiropractic clinic in Knoxville, where I ended up for almost two years. They said they would work with me as far as payment was concerned. Somewhat skeptical, but having nothing to lose and no money, I began going every day, then every other day, then eventually twice a week.

In the beginning, I sometimes drove the 60-mile round-trip twice a day until after I moved into Knoxville. It helped, but I really didn't start feeling better until I began seeing a physical therapist and a massage therapist as well. Throughout the year, we battled the pinched nerve-whiplash type problems that appeared after the fall.

A dentist made a plastic splint for me to wear in my mouth constantly, which, along with medication and physical therapy, eventually helped with the jaw problems, called TMJ.

My arm and neck got better over time but even now I would rather go through childbirth several times than repeat what I went through that year.

Eventually, the other physical problems improved as well. I even went dancing at the scene of the accident again, where they secretly videotaped me because by now we were in a full-fledged lawsuit. For someone who had led aerobics classes for her friends in Utah and danced and sang her way through performances, it was natural to go dancing.

I wasn't trying to hide anything. I was just happy to be able to move again!

I never saw the tape, but I'm sure it shows someone happily dancing her heart out, someone used to being physically active, in touch with her body and music. I was desperately trying to get back to normal.

I was also in a state of denial.

Having developed a tendency to push myself hard, I felt if I ignored things, maybe they would go away. After all, the show must go on.

And I didn't *want* anything to be wrong with me - I had enough stuff wrong with the ear problems, Crohn's disease, bronchitis, asthma and pneumonia from childhood. I was allergic to everything, bit my fingernails and was very nearsighted. Wasn't that enough?

In June, within weeks after the accident, I went back to school, using my scholarship and VA grant. In spite of doing well in the extremely competitive communications department at the University of Utah and an almost straight-A average so far in grad school at Tennessee, I flunked out and didn't really know why. I wasn't able to concentrate, my vision sometimes blurred when I read, and I couldn't seem to organize or even understand my assignments.

At the time of the accident I had been playing keyboards with a local band. Having played my grandmother's old-fashioned piano since before I was tall enough to climb up onto the stool and long before Tumbleweed Rock, it was second nature for me to form the chord patterns and make my fingers dance across the keys. I played by ear, almost on autopilot.

During the first job I had playing music after the accident, I had trouble physically forming chords and finger positions with my right hand; I couldn't do certain leads and instinctively knew my timing was off but couldn't seem to correct it.

Even worse, I couldn't seem to *remember* certain chord progressions, leads, lyrics – or sometimes entire songs. Looking at our current repertoire, I felt familiar with only about half of the song titles. It was becoming apparent that at least some parts of my memory were simply not functioning

I stared at the black and white keys, then walked off the stage in the middle of a song. In music, as I was now feeling about life in general, I felt out of step and a beat or so behind.

The band fired me soon after - (a first) so I put away my keyboard and didn't want anything to do with music for the first time in my life.

Strangely, I didn't care all that much. I didn't really care about much of anything and found it impossible to think ahead or plan. I felt like I existed in a vacuum and nothing was real.

My formerly immaculate home went to pieces. I was having nightmares and seemed to need a lot more sleep than ever before. I also had trouble with temperature. I would be cold when everyone else was hot and vice versa.

My son and I, formerly close, began to have differences and he told me I'd changed. He blamed the TV accident - and does to this day. I clung to the belief that I was fine. The rest of the world was crazy, including him.

I moved to Knoxville but abandoned my job hunt. I was having trouble getting through an interview because I was having trouble talking.

Me - the communication major, the actress, the corporate trainer, the speaker - was having a problem literally forming the right words. Concerning talking, it was like I needed a road map. I knew where I wanted to go but didn't know how to get there. The words wouldn't come out of my mouth correctly.

Sometimes I slurred my words or stuttered, especially in unfamiliar or stressful situations. It was as though a computer in my brain had malfunctioned or short-circuited. At the time I tried to blame it on the jaw problem or the splint.

My sense of time, direction and distance didn't seem to be intact either.

Formerly known for an uncanny sense of direction, I had traveled the West on band gigs without much more than a passing glance at road signs and maps. Now I got lost and disoriented in stores, parking lots, on highways and even in familiar neighborhoods.

I had several close calls while driving and had also gotten very clumsy, something with which I still have problems, especially picking up small objects and seemingly tripping over my own feet. The two middle fingers on my right hand were still a real problem.

That natural alarm clock that often wakes one up spontaneously just before the bedside alarm goes off no longer worked. Other things about me were different too. These seemingly little things added up to a big change.

Where I used to be Ms. Personality, the life of the party and a bubbly extrovert with lots of friends, activities and interests, I now didn't really like to leave the house. I had trouble with small talk and mingling and had the attention span of a gnat. When I did try to be the outgoing entertainer I used to be, I felt like I was trying to be someone else and in danger of forgetting my lines.

I spaced out often and felt fuzzy-headed most of the time, as though I'd forgotten something important - and often I had. Sometimes it felt as though I had lost my capacity for thinking at all, and I felt like an impartial observer of my own life.

My hearing seemed worse than it was before and sometimes I felt as if I were moving in slow motion or underwater.

I used to be a somewhat hyperactive overachiever, but I could now sit for hours and do absolutely nothing - and not even realize it.

The seemingly simple act of following instructions baffled me and I was rendered helpless by all but the most basic recipe or "assembly required" label.

When I could regularly drive again without pain, I would catch myself speeding a lot. It felt like I had no natural sense of how fast (or slow) I was going if there were no other cars around or I didn't look constantly at the speedometer.

I was stopped by a police officer one night coming home from the VA hospital in Nashville where I'd been treated for Crohn's disease. Since it was quite late, he asked if I'd been drinking. I truthfully replied that I hadn't. He had me get out of the car and walk from point A to point B.

Tired, sick and my balance being off from the aforementioned inner ear problem, I had a little trouble. He then asked me to count backward from 100.

"100...99...98...." was as far as I got before I realized that I just didn't know what came next – I had *no idea.* It felt as though there was nothing at all in my brain at that exact moment. I may as well have been asleep.

Looking blankly at the officer, I tried to explain that I was just tired and sick. After showing him my still intact hospital wristband and brand new prescriptions, luckily, he let me go with a warning, but it shook me up. Now I felt like I really *was* a dumb blonde, a stereotypical character and recurring role for me in my acting career.

In the past, I had developed an ability to deal with major ongoing stress, but it seemed that I could now deal with nothing. It felt as though life was a carousel and I was waiting for it to slow down so I could hop on again, but it never did.

What was WRONG with me? My entire life was spiraling downward. I stayed confused and didn't have any idea what to do about it as the months went by.

Standing outside in a cold rain watching traffic one day, I wondered who I had become. It dawned on me that I literally didn't have the sense enough to come in out of the rain.

After I had trouble playing the piano and typing because of the dysfunctional fingers on my right hand, an acquaintance eventually referred me to Dr. Robert Chironna with the Patricia Neal Rehabilitation Center.

At that first appointment in March of 1993, already more than a year after the TV set incident, he asked many questions. Was I having trouble sleeping? Anything unusual about my vision? Were there any memory problems? Did I have trouble following directions?

I couldn't see the significance of this line of questioning, which seemed unrelated to the problem with my two fingers, but his inquiries hit home. Most of my answers were yes.

He had me do some simple maneuvers in the office. Stand up. Touch my nose. Walk. He asked point blank if I'd been in any sort of accident where I might have sustained a head injury.

"Hmmm…Nooo, not that I can think of," I replied, my mind off in outer space somewhere, wondering how he knew I had trouble following simple directions and what that had to do with the two fingers on my right hand.

He asked more questions, and I could relate to each one. He checked my reflexes. He checked my reflexes again. My right leg stuck straight out each time.

More questions. How did this doctor know *everything* that was going on with me, and what did it have to do with my two malfunctioning digits? I was amazed and confused. His questions triggered frustration at the state in which I had found myself over the past year.

Tears were now streaming down my face, and my emotions were all over the place as he gently asked again if I were *sure* I hadn't had a head injury at some point.

I had been thinking in terms of *car accidents* when it suddenly dawned on me that I'd been knocked unconscious by a falling TV set just over a year ago. I guess that could have been considered a head injury… Duh.

In retrospect, complaining about my two fingers when I had a head injury was like complaining about a splinter when one has a gunshot wound.

I learned that the numbness and tingling in my fingers and hand was due to a brain injury, not a pinched nerve as I had previously thought, and that the residual effects of even a mild head injury can manifest in some surprising and unsettling ways.

I learned that 1.4 million people sustain Traumatic Brain Injury in the United States each year. Out of that number, 50,000 die, 235,000 are hospitalized; and 1.1 million are treated and released from hospital emergency departments. I was told that about 85 percent of recovery takes place within six months of the onset of the injury, and I learned that I was almost a textbook case. I wished I had gotten help before, but no one, including me, had recognized the problem. (Statistics from the Brain Injury Association of America.)

Sent for counseling and more testing, I was put on medication and played computer games designed to help with things like hand-eye coordination during outpatient therapy. The staff was friendly and helpful. I was grateful. Through this kind and supportive health care team, I learned that I was not going crazy, that my symptoms were quite common for those who had suffered head trauma and that I was not alone. I felt like I was slowly crawling out of some sort of hole and seeing a tiny bit of light at last, but it was to be a long road to recovery.

Chapter 14

Drifting

And through it all she offers me protection
A lot of love and affection
Whether I'm right or wrong
And down the waterfall
Wherever it may take me
I know that life won't break me
When I come to call
She won't forsake me
I'm loving angels instead.

- Angels, Robbie Williams

There were some bright spots with the memory loss. For instance, I could look at the same magazine month after month and still retain interest because except for an occasional deja-vu-like flashback, I wouldn't remember seeing it. Television reruns were no problem. It was impossible for me to hold a grudge because soon I forgot what I was upset about in the first place, unless I was reminded.

Things I liked before I didn't necessarily like now and vice versa.

Clothes, decor, tastes and interests had all changed. Incredibly, even my food preferences and handwriting changed.

A childhood spelling bee winner, I now had a great deal of trouble spelling even simple words.

I couldn't seem to coordinate my clothes like I used to and while sitting in church once, I looked down to find myself wearing two mismatched shoes of the same color. I often found the tags and seams on the *outside* of my clothes, to my embarrassment and for some reason, I had a great deal of trouble applying lip and eye liner.

I could even get through a battery of tests if they were not too long or involved.

I could usually bluff my way through short-term situations or circumstances but if anything got complicated, I couldn't handle it. My brain just seemed to shut off.

After a while I learned to cover very well though. Having a performance background, I still knew perception meant everything and most of the time I could usually sustain the *appearance* of everything being fine, at least temporarily. Somehow, it seemed important to maintain this external front and I was so confused, I didn't know what else to do.

This ability to present a normal facade turned out to be a double-edged sword. On the outside, I appeared to be the same person. People still had the same expectations of me and made the same demands. On the inside, I was completely different.

My symptoms were inconsistent and invisible. No one else knew when my vision went haywire in the middle of a page or I momentarily forgot where I was or what I was doing. No one realized that my speech was hesitant because I couldn't form the words. They just thought I was thinking and carefully choosing my words or framing what I was about to say.

No one knew of my confusion as I tried to organize my thoughts, find memories and process information.

Where there used to be an innate sense of right and wrong and an internalized set of standards based on values, reason and personal priorities, there now seemed to be nothing but habit and rote. For instance, I knew that I made a decision not to drink or do drugs, but I couldn't quite remember why I made that decision.

I often felt like a zombie with no sound judgment or depth of emotion.

"Flooding," I had learned, was a term used when head injury patients feel cognitively overwhelmed. Thoughts become like alphabet soup, jumbled and mixed up, which was exactly how I felt much of the time.

I completely lost touch with friends and relatives I was formerly close to, I'm sure they didn't understand, because I didn't. After I moved to Knoxville, I even grew apart from Blondie. It didn't occur to me to develop any kind of social life or support system. I was simply existing from day to day. It wasn't that I felt animosity toward anyone or anything – I just felt nothing and initiated nothing.

In my case, there seemed to be no area of my life that had not been touched by that bump on the head because the very core of my personality had been affected. My spirituality, sexuality, employability, intellect and emotions were all different.

I went through the motions of life as it used to be because it was what I knew. For instance, I used to read regularly. After the accident, I still tried to read at my regular time just before going to bed at night. When I realized that I got no pleasure or satisfaction in any way from it; I just abandoned trying. It was the same with going to church, shopping and countless other daily life activities.

I couldn't play or write music or poetry to express myself because it felt like there was no "self" to express.

After withdrawing from college, messing up the music on stage, not finding another job and becoming isolated, my confidence plummeted, and I sank into a profound depression. It felt like I was living in a world with no color, only shades of gray.

While I waited for the old me to return, I stumbled and fell countless times, missed appointments, screwed up my checkbook, stayed confused, didn't pay bills on time, had horrible headaches and mood swings, needed at least 12 or more hours of sleep at night and battled thoughts of depression and occasionally, suicide.

Dr. Chironna put me on anti-depressants and I was put in touch with a support group for TBI victims that I never attended. I spoke with several members but had no interest in associating with this or any other group.

I didn't know what I wanted to do with my life now, but selfishly thought I didn't want to spend the rest of it being a "poster child" for a disability I wasn't ready to accept. I just wanted to forget about TBI and forget that it ever affected me. Reluctantly, however, I had to admit that it did help to know I was not alone.

Social Security disability was mentioned, but even though I needed money, it would have been a tiny check and somewhere down deep inside it felt too much like giving up. I still didn't want to admit that anything was wrong. I eventually applied half-heartedly and was turned down the first time. I didn't apply again until much later.

I've dealt with physical problems all of my life, but I just couldn't deal with the possibility of a screw being loose, as they say. I kept hoping it would get better. I still had the feeling that I was waiting for the old me to come back. I didn't feel like I knew or liked this new person inhabiting my body.

I wished I could have broken something. Broken bones eventually heal. I didn't know if broken minds did. The medical community at the time generally believed that if the brain were going to regenerate at all, it would do so within two years of the injury. If that were the case, there wasn't much hope for me. More than a year had already gone by before I even found out what was wrong.

The lawsuit dragged on, and I didn't have enough money to live on, with only the VA income. At a deposition, an attorney asked me what was still bothering me. My first inclination was to shout *"Everything – where do I begin?"* But I couldn't find the right words to explain something I didn't quite understand myself.

I still had trouble finding words, period.

Eventually, I began to feel better physically. I had given up attempting any activities of a physical nature such as exercising or dancing. I just didn't do much at all anymore. I never went anywhere. When I wasn't sleeping, I wandered aimlessly about the house.

Vaguely, it occurred to me that I still needed a job. Our financial situation was becoming dire.

I was not disfigured and gave every appearance of functioning at a high level, but I knew I couldn't do the same kind of work for which I had been preparing throughout my college career. I still couldn't speak very well and "flooded" easily.

We were way behind on rent and about to be evicted.

In a feeble attempt to give Brian some stability, I rented him a cheap room with a community bath near his high school. I put most of my belongings in a storage unit and began sleeping in my car.

I didn't have sense enough to be afraid as I jockeyed my car into a position where the parking lot lights wouldn't be directly in my eyes. I alternated between Kroger and Wal-mart parking lots and began looking for a job again but didn't know what I could do. I used their rest rooms as well as nearby service stations to clean up in the mornings. I ate the cheapest food at any restaurant within range, often stocking up on crackers from the salad bar for my evening meal.

I couldn't think ahead any farther than that and seemed capable of only living in the moment. Planning for a future - immediate or distant - was an abstract concept that I couldn't quite grasp.

Going home to Mom and Dad's didn't occur to me, nor did the thought of going to any friends or relatives. I could no longer hear the call of the mountains or the peace and hope they once represented. In my current world, they didn't even exist. I lived from day to day in an aimless existence with no hope, no dreams, and no goals, feeling very little, going through the motions of life. But one day, I felt cold, as temperatures dropped in East Tennessee.

That fall, I went to the Volunteers of America homeless shelter in Knoxville where I found a more comfortable, warmer and probably safer sleeping place than the driver's seat. I was at least among people again on a regular basis.

At the family shelter, there were all sizes, shapes and colors of women and children. My roommate was a young black girl who was trying to overcome addiction problems through spirituality. Another woman had Crohn's disease and one night lost control of her bowels right on the floor outside my door. Apparently she couldn't get into the community bathroom fast enough.

Some residents seemed angry. Some seemed confused. Many appeared frustrated and several seemed to have given up hope. I was a silent but interested observer.

There were rules, some of which I couldn't remember. There was a community dining room where we ate. The food left a lot to be desired, but at least it was something.

Like so long ago at the Florence Crittenton Home, there were no close relationships and residence there felt very temporary.

Homelessness knows no boundaries, and I felt sorry for these folks. Many were there through no fault of their own. Some seemed deeply troubled to be there at all while others seemed not to care where they were. Perhaps I should have felt sorry for myself but I didn't even have the presence of mind to feel self-pity. But at least I felt something.

The intake counselors at the shelter wondered, after they filled out my history, what I was doing there with so much education and experience. I didn't seem to have any substance abuse problems or obvious physical limitations and appeared to be fine. I wondered what I was doing there myself, but I had no answers.

Chapter 15

The Roselady

Just remember in the winter, far beneath the bitter snows
lies the seed that with the sun's love
in the spring becomes the rose.

- The Rose, Bette Midler

At some point I was able to get an apartment with my parents' help, but I was still desperate for a job.

Answering an ad in the newspaper, in late 1994 I began working for a woman who sent me out selling roses on weekends in nightclubs. I had first seen this in Las Vegas many years ago when a very glamorous woman wearing a modified tuxedo had gone from table to table with a basket of roses in a club. Several people bought me roses at that time, sending them up to the "girl in the band."

But here in East Tennessee, some of the outlying areas I drove to were almost three hours away from each other. The locale varied from week to week. I paid my own expenses and made $1 a rose. Not a very lucrative position, it was still my only offer.

Since I was accustomed to the nightclub scene from playing music, the atmosphere didn't really bother me, and, surprisingly, I had enough sense to know how to market myself. I still had flashy clothes and Dolly Parton-style wigs in storage that I utilized. All I had to do was walk in with a basket of roses, attract attention and everyone would flock to me with cash in hand, I hoped. And for the most part, it worked.

Most of these clubs in the rural areas of East Tennessee didn't have fancy brass fittings, ferns or stemware. They had neon, guitar-shaped signs, big dance floors, miniscule toilet stalls that didn't always lock, and lots of pick-up trucks in the parking lot, although a few had a sophisticated ambiance and clientele that would rival their big-city counterparts.

Even though I had been in many similar places in the past while playing music, I was a little intimidated my first time out as a rose salesperson, still lacking confidence and not yet adjusted to the brain injury. I stood stupidly in the small, muted vestibule with my basket of roses and finally, taking a step inside, was immediately approached by a young man in a ball cap.

"Got some flares…?" he asked over the noise and loud music.

"What?" I yelled back.

"Flares, I need some flares….how much?" he shouted.

"I don't have any flares," I said. "All I've got are roses. What do you need flares for? Is your car broke down?" A flare, as far as I knew, was something you lit and placed along the roadside in case of emergency.

"You do *too* have flares, rat thar, see….?"he said, pointing to my basket.

"No, really, I don't, I only have roses in here, lifting the basket and shuffling the stems so he could plainly see what was in there. "What would someone need flares for in here?"

"Fer mah girlfrend. She lahks flares, lots of 'em…." He said as he began checking out my roses one by one.

"Oh, *roses*, you mean *roses*, that's what you want…." I said, now catching on that his pronounced mountain dialect was so thick that "flowers" had become "flares" to my Yankee ears.

❧

Each patron was different. There were those with style, class and intelligence in their eyes. There were those with an air of superiority. Some came merely to observe. There were the Jerry Springer refugees and others who came just to let off steam.

These were not what one would call "sophisticated" crowds, for the most part, although it depended on the club. Young and old came just to dance or to abuse the substance of their choice, and some came simply by accident or default, like the lost trucker, who, with a woman in tow, didn't know where else to go.

"Gimme *two* of them!! 'Ahm a ro-man-tic sonofabitch!!" declared the burly, hairy Neanderthal as I came into his line of vision. His date, an empty chair, was apparently in the rest room.

"Yes, sir! Would you like yellow or red?" I asked pleasantly. Later, on the dance floor, a woman at his side clutching the flowers smiled at me. She was missing two teeth in front, had a bald patch on her scalp and a lazy eye. I smiled back.

Some of the clubs were nicer than others, but most were rowdy and rough. I began gauging the nights by the number of barroom brawls. Any more than a three-fight-night usually meant fewer rose sales. People were distracted by the blood.

I sidestepped prone bodies in parking lots, their hands often loosely clutching a bottle or cigarettes. I watched the dancers inside with their wildly suggestive gyrations that left nothing to the imagination. I avoided the marijuana smoke emanating from certain tables and cars, all the while gingerly clutching my basket of "flares."

Neighboring states had dry counties, where alcohol was not sold and there were no night clubs, so residents crossed the state line to "raze a little hail!"

Crowds came for a girls' night out - or they might have been celebrating something specific like a birthday, anniversary or divorce.

Patrons came in all shapes, sizes and ages. Depending on the venue, some appeared unkempt with hair that looked dirty and many women wore sparkly or tight clothing that showed lots of skin. Among the men, suits or button-down shirts were rare, blue jeans were standard and there was an occasional cowboy hat amongst the sea of ball caps.

Sometimes there were some really classy folks, but I had the feeling that they were visiting from somewhere else. Ethnic diversity didn't exist except for one establishment that was considered very progressive and appealing to the younger crowd.

The bands were loud, wild Southern rockers, with some country and recorded hip-hop thrown in on breaks. The Turner Brothers Band was legendary in these parts, and rightfully so. Their tight sound reflected the attitude of the working man on a Saturday night and served as a release for the week's daily grind. Inhibitions went out the door as they launched into *Honk-Tonk Woman*, or anything by Lynyrd Skynyrd.

The Starlight Club in Greene County had for years been the only place to party for miles and there was a different Starlight Club in Campbell County. Other stops represented a hodgepodge of VFWs, American Legions, biker bars, cocktail lounges, strip joints and more.

This was where the action was on weekends and it unfolded like a theatrical production with comedy, drama, defined characters and human interest.

Patrons would call out to their friends, whistle and respond to the band's prompting with rebel yells. Some of them I could barely understand because of the accent. Others I could barely understand because they were slurring their words, usually, I surmised, an effect of whatever substance they were abusing at the moment. But they all danced their hearts out, they were friendly, and, more importantly, they bought roses.

Chivalry and romance are not dead. They live in the heart of every redneck in those hills. Males and females bought roses, especially when the females realized that this showy blonde was no threat. Women bought lots of roses on Thursdays in Claiborne County - 'ladies' night.' Sometimes they kept them for themselves. Sometimes they asked me to deliver them to a man across the room. Shrinking violets they weren't.

In reality, these people were the salt of the earth. Most were real, caring, down-home country folk, without airs or pretense and I came to treasure them. Hard-working and plain-spoken, they were just out to have a little fun and blow off some steam on the weekend.

They may not have realized it, but the sometimes trashy clothes, wild dancing, even the occasional fights were all part of an elaborate mating ritual, reflecting different levels of a socioeconomic caste system.

This was a unique culture - one that was honest and straightforward but one that could be unflinchingly compassionate or brutal in equal measures. I seemed to bring out the former and tried to ignore the latter.

I became one of my employer's best salespeople and actually began to enjoy it. Something about the long drives at night left room for lots of thinking and eventually praying. A person can get a heck of a lot of religion speeding alone over Clinch Mountain or down Jellico Mountain in a snowstorm at midnight.

Speeding was necessary because there was a limited window of opportunity for rose sales. If I came too early, people wouldn't pay the price. If I came too late, they were too drunk to stand.

Sometimes I hurried to make more sales, sometimes I stayed and danced a few dances. I drove all over East Tennessee and calculated just how much chocolate and Coca-cola I needed to stay alert enough to get safely home around 5 a.m., dropping off the basket and any leftover roses on my boss's doorstep.

Welcomed into the clubs by all, I treated each person with respect and excellence in customer service. Helping them find the exact rose they wanted, I would deliver it with a message if requested. I assisted with color selection as well as occasionally offering an opinion on something, when asked. There were regular customers, and I made friends.

Eventually, cautiously, I even played a few songs or sang harmony with some of the bands along the route. As my confidence grew, I even tried new material.

Throughout much of the mid-1990s, people looked for the "Rose Lady" and came to expect that small touch of class and civility at certain establishments.

I attracted so much male attention that I had unofficial bodyguards looking out the windows discreetly when I left to make sure I got to my car safely. I would turn, smile and wave, then happily drive off to the next stop.

If someone was a regular customer or bought a dozen roses, I felt they deserved a deal occasionally, but my boss was adamantly opposed to this marketing and public relations move. So I found a florist who was willing to sell me a few roses for under a dollar apiece. I took these with me on my route and gave them away myself in those situations and occasionally just to someone I felt was deserving.

Soon, my boss found out about this and became angry, accusing me of stealing her business. I was fired. She also made threats, saying that if she ever caught me out selling roses in one of her clubs, she would sue me, cut my tires and have somebody waiting in the parking lot for me.

Shocked, stunned and weeping, the next weekend I gathered my wits and bought a number of my cheap roses at the florist. I wasn't planning to sell them, but she couldn't stop me from giving them away. I wanted to say goodbye to all my friends on the route.

I had been a regular fixture for almost two years now. The musicians, club owners, customers and doormen who had all treated me so well deserved an explanation of some kind.

I didn't make much money selling roses (sometimes I even lost money), but it got me out of the house and had become my social life as well.

Deciding to go straight to where my favorite band and club owners were, I could party and dance all night now that I wasn't working. When I got there, I tearfully began giving out roses to people, telling them I had been fired and probably wouldn't be back. When they pressed for details, I poured out my heart and told the whole story to the owners, who already felt like family to me.

Looking at each other, they almost simultaneously said,

"We want *you* to be our rose lady. Why don't you just start your own business and come up here?"

I told them of my former employer's malicious threats and that I couldn't possibly do that. I was truly afraid of her. They laughed, saying they'd just dump her in the river, and I had no doubt that these good ole boys from the back country would do just that.

I stayed and danced the night away, but had no plans to run afoul of my former employer at that point.

Chapter 16

Honky-Tonk heroes and a home

I played a divorcee in New York City,
I had to put up some kind of a fight.
The lady then she covered me with roses,
She blew my nose and then she blew my mind.

- Honky-Tonk Woman, The Rolling Stones

The next week, I went to another one of my stops and spoke with the owner, security person and the doorman. I figured my replacement would be heading in that direction, and I wanted to tell them all goodbye and explain.

My boss had told me she had exclusive arrangements with all of these places, but it turned out that she had no such thing. They, too, wanted only me to be their "rose lady" and told me I was welcome *any time.*

Having no desire to see my former boss dumped into the river, I still needed an income. After thinking about it for about a month and getting desperate and hungry, I got a business license, tax number, found a wholesaler and began my own route. I was no longer afraid of my former employer and never saw any replacements coming around. I made a little more money this way and gradually added more stops. I was working now across five counties.

I listened to music and also discovered audio books. Reading was no longer enjoyable for me since the head injury and I had never liked watching television or movies much, but I became hooked on recorded books. They made the miles fly by! Each weekend, I followed a long stretch of highway into the night, listening to a book or music, leaving my cares and worries behind. The sounds of rock 'n' roll, bluegrass and the southern gospel I learned at my Dad's knee accompanied me from Greeneville to Jellico. Steve Earle, Emmylou Harris, Rod Stewart and I logged a lot of miles together.

Selling roses wasn't all fun and games, however. I would start early and pick up the roses, which had to be refrigerated. There was no room in my refrigerator for food even if I could have afforded it. Then a small, plastic, individual water container had to be filled with water and affixed to the stem of each rose, a lengthy process which usually involved wrestling with leaves and thorns. My fingers were usually bleeding slightly by the time I got done with this procedure. Finally, I loaded them into my beribboned basket, and away I went.

Customers came looking for the rose lady and often confided in me. They told me their problems in rest rooms and parking lots. They shared good news, bad news and holidays with me. I took special orders and added Teddy bears and Easter bunnies to my basket occasionally.

I made bouquets from bunches the wholesaler was ready to throw out, assured that they would last at least another week. I became known as the "Mother Teresa" of the Sundowner Club. I sang karaoke for the first time in a Bulls Gap biker bar where, much to my own amazement, I began remembering the words to songs again! I was re-learning to play the keyboards whenever I sat in as a guest with bands and was cheered whenever I got onstage at either Starlight. I was even instrumental in three marriage proposals!

Most of the men were gentlemen and the women were ladies, at least around me, except for a young man at one of my last stops. Every time I saw him, he was drunk and obnoxious. Not just to me, but to other women as well. We usually just tried to ignore him as he made obscene gestures and followed us around.

One night, after I had been selling roses for several years, I was a little on edge and tired when I turned and there he was making gross, embarrassing and suggestive gestures. Never had I been anything less than professional and courteous while out on the job. I just stared at him for a minute.

Suddenly, in that moment, he completely infuriated me.

No one had ever seen the rose lady upset before, but I stuck a finger in his face and pounded his chest, pushing him backward and blasting forth with a dressing down so severe the devil would have been proud, right in front of everybody.

He was now drunkenly cowering, backing toward the door. I continued my tirade at the top of my voice, oblivious to the scene I was causing even over the noise of the crowd. Once we reached the door, I jerked it open and told him to "get the hell out and don't come back until you learn a little respect."

It wasn't my job or even my club, but I turned around to see stunned onlookers including the bouncers and the owners, apparently right behind me all along, who burst into applause! The club owners were laughing.

"Way to go, Roselady!"

"I'm glad you did that!"

"He deserved it, good job!"

The next time I saw the young man he apologized and he was no trouble ever again.

Late one night I was the first one at the scene of a semi-truck accident on the two-lane highway leading out of Claiborne County. Thinking of my father driving a truck for all those years, I directed traffic, got someone to telephone for help, then cradled the shaking and bleeding driver in a blanket in my arms, talking with him until help arrived. No one at the bars noticed the blood on my evening gown.

Another time, two of my best and biggest customers came to me dragging a hapless, bedraggled, little man between them. Standing before me, they not-so-gently nudged him.

"Tell 'er," one of my burly friends said to him through clenched teeth, eyes still on me.

"Yeah, right now," said the other strapping young man.

"What??" I asked, alarmed. I thought maybe he had run into my vehicle, parked outside.

" I…I…" began the drunken wreck of a soul between the two linebackers.

"Go ahead," again through the clenched teeth of the one on the right, jerking the man in the middle slightly.

"Well…." he began again, faltering.

The hulk on the left took it upon himself to help the poor fellow out.

"Roselady," he said nobly, "this man stoled a rose from you. He slided it out the back of yer basket when yew didn't notice."

"Yeah, we saw 'im do it," the other chimed in. Scenes from the movie *Deliverance* flashed through my mind.

I didn't know what to say. I was feeling very sorry for the little fellow, who didn't have much going for him anyway, and, for all I knew, they had taken justice upon themselves out in the parking lot already judging from his appearance. Or maybe he just always looked that way. You couldn't really tell in this territory.

"He's gonna pay yew for it," said hulk No. 2.

"That's right," agreed No. 1.

"That's right," mumbled the disheveled little man in an indignant and slurred voice. "I was gonna pay fer it, like they said…"

"If you needed a rose that badly, I would have given you one," I said, genuinely concerned. "You keep your money," I told him as he fumbled around in a pocket for a couple of dollars with his captors still holding on to him.

With a hangdog look, he said, "I'm sorry, miss... I didn't mean to… You take this," and thrust a wad of bills at me. "Puh-leeze, take this."

One of the enforcers grabbed the bills and held them out to me righteously.

I finally took one bill and put the rest in the little man's hand, closing his fist around them tightly, smiling at him. With this, they let him go.

After praising my vigilantes profusely and extolling the virtues of both honesty and compassion, I disappeared into the rest room for a while, not sure whether to laugh or cry.

Johnny and Arnold were the club owners who had encouraged me to start my own business in the first place. Without their friendship and support, I would not have had the courage to continue. I thought of them as family.

Another club owner ordered flowers from me weekly. Still another fed me almost every night on the route. I got to know the police and state troopers who stopped me regularly for speeding, usually letting me go with a warning, although I racked up quite a few tickets during this period of my life.

No one ever mistreated me in any way. I dodged darts, pool cues, barmaids, drunken drivers, possums in the road and an occasional would-be suitor.

Men sometimes asked me out, but I rarely went and they just accepted it with good-natured grace. Most just looked and acted a bit shy. Sometimes they wanted to know if I was available.

"Ewe murried?' they would ask.

"No, I'm a widow. My husband died." I would reply.

"Ewe kill 'im?" they inquired politely, in all seriousness.

This earnest, matter-of-fact conversation happened at least three times.

There were a few men whom I would have liked to know better and would have gone out with, but I didn't want to shatter their illusions. Appearance still counted and the reality was that the ethereal presence they saw with the roses in the dimly lit clubs was not what I looked like when I awoke in the morning. Like in show business, it was all smoke and mirrors. I couldn't risk someone falling for the image and being disappointed.

Some guys put dollar bills in my basket for no reason. Some said they had only come out that night to see me. A few bought entire baskets of roses and even wanted to buy the basket. Some bought the rose lady a rose. Women continued to buy almost as many.

Not all residents of East Tennessee were like these honky-tonk heroes and heroines, but it is to them that I owe a debt of gratitude. They took care of me. Out there in hillbilly territory, I eventually learned to accept myself for who I was and to have faith that all would work out as it was meant to. I learned not to worry. I had conversations with God, with Lynn and with myself. I prayed.

For more than five years, I felt angels' wings helping me through white-knuckle driving conditions. In Union County, I felt the spirit of my father's ancestors watching over me. Driving miles in the dark, I often felt a protective, calming presence beside me in the passenger seat so real it was almost tangible. I felt very safe and was learning to relax and feel joy again.

A single flower came to signify hope for me, and the people who bought them will never know how they changed my life.

After the head injury but before I began selling roses, I had become a recluse without even realizing it, shutting myself off from the world. My emotions were flat, and I had lost my sense of humor as well as my sense of direction. Nothing had been funny to me in a long while, whether a direct result of the head injury or the subsequent depression.

One night, without an audio book to listen to, I stopped at a truck stop in search of the western, romance or biography I favored. This particular place didn't carry audio books but in their CD/cassette music section, I found some comedy selections. Having nothing to lose, I bought several and went on my way.

Halfheartedly listening to the first comedian, something struck me as laugh-out-loud funny for the first time since I could remember.

Specifics elude me now, so many years later, but it was so funny to me at the time, I had to pull over to the side of the road. I was laughing so hard, tears were rolling down my cheeks and I thought I might wet my pants!

It felt wonderful. The tension of the past several years disappeared as relief washed over me in the form of almost hysterical laughter. This was the first time I had an inkling that I might be getting better, and from that point on my attitude changed ever so slightly. Humor, something many of us take for granted, had crept back into my life.

The rose money was fairly steady. I wouldn't get rich but I could survive this way, at least for a while. More importantly, it gave me confidence. I will always be grateful to those who bought my roses and the club owners who welcomed me, more than they would ever realize.

Since I only worked weekends, I was free during the week. Very cautiously, I signed up for another graduate class thinking that maybe I could pick up where I left off in school. It was like testing the water with your toes before taking a bath each time I signed up for a class. I would speak with the instructor, look at the syllabus and check out the textbooks.

Slowly, and with the help of some very understanding professors and disabled student services, I began working toward my master's degree again. Silly as it sounds, I had to re-learn how to learn!

The cognitive processes that most of us take for granted are actually rather complicated. And quite by accident, I stumbled into a class where Dr. Katherine Greenberg had developed building blocks and a model designed to help students learn. Others were applying the program to their classrooms and to their young students. I was applying it to myself.

It was around this time that I decided I'd like a home of my own.

Hoping that someday the lawsuit would be settled and I might have at least enough money for a down payment on something, I was looking at property around the university. After all, I was a student. I also thought I'd like to find a home with an extra apartment, like a duplex, which might help my house pay for itself and eventually provide me with an income. At least I was thinking again. I reasoned that any place close to the university would always have renters and found a small four-plex, but the deal fell through.

I turned to Dad for help, promising him any money from the lawsuit, and kept looking. I spoke to Realtors and other landlords in the area. I learned from everyone I talked to and made friends with folks in the rental business. At least I was making friends again.

Through one of them, in the fall of '96, I heard about a property that was still in probate and almost on campus! I hunted for the address and found a gray, deserted, two-story elephant of a house, windows and doors boarded up and hiding behind an overgrowth of trees and brush.

Although I had driven by it many times, I hadn't even noticed it.

After carefully poking around the exterior of the house and yard, where a huge tree threatened the roof, I tracked down the attorney who persuaded the executors of the estate to let me see the inside. Bringing along a friend who was a contractor, we all stood silently by as the plywood was pulled off one of the doors.

Inside were piles of trash and debris from someone's life. Clothes, dishes, old cans of food, detergent, tattered chairs and mattresses littered the floors and counters. We found ham radio equipment, pictures, Christmas decorations and old toilets.

Graffiti was on some of the walls upstairs, and pieces of the ceiling were gone. There were holes in the floor upstairs and some of the plaster on the walls appeared to be crumbling. But there was a basement and sturdy hardwood floors downstairs that were, for the most part, in good condition.

With both a front and back porch, leaded glass around the front door and high ceilings, I could see beyond the wreckage. I could envision the spirit of a great past in this old house that had already been divided into a four-plex.

I talked Dad into buying it, sight unseen, for very little because it was in such bad shape. But when Mom and Dad came down to close the deal, some of the selling party got cold feet and changed their minds. The judge had already ordered them to sell the property, so eventually the transaction was completed.

It just seemed that nothing in my life ever went smoothly.

When Dad got his first look at the place, he couldn't see anything but the mess and left almost physically ill. Not a visionary, he never wanted to be a landlord either. For a very long time he wasn't a happy camper about the whole thing, but the property was in his name and he took responsibility for the renovations.

He tried to direct the project from Wisconsin, trusting my contractor friend Jay and making infrequent site visits.

I had dated Jay on and off, so I knew he had done insurance work and respected his opinions. He had looked at the place initially before we bought it, saying he thought he could do something with it. After agreeing on a price, Dad gave him money to begin the undertaking.

We started on the first floor. Work was slow, and they had to haul dumpsters full of junk away. I was impatient. Daily, I would go see what had been done. I also took a job at a nonprofit organization near campus around this time.

As director of volunteers for an art organization, I was in charge of recruiting and training people for what I found to be a stuffy, unfriendly place to work. There was an atmosphere of snobbery, and I was having trouble relating to the rest of the staff. The previous person in my position had left the department in shambles, with no organization or records, no solid programs and very little training of existing volunteers. There had been much staff turnover and I came to be one of those that "turned over" as well, leaving of my own accord after less than a year.

I was still dealing with the head injury, restoring the house, selling roses on weekends, having some problems with the Crohn's disease and taking classes. That was enough.

Jay had one studio apartment done, so we rented that to a graduate student who appeared on our doorstep during renovations begging for accommodations.

I tried to help Jay and his crew as they worked on another part of the building. When it was almost finished, I moved in. I bought furniture and hung pictures. We had no heat yet, but now it began to look like something special. Even Dad could recognize its unique character and beauty now.

I found a secondhand piano, Victorian Christmas ornaments and a glass topped dining set for my formal dining room. We hung a porch swing from the front porch, and that Christmas I decked the halls with three Christmas trees and the sound of carols on my stereo.

We kept waiting for Jay to come back and begin work on the second floor, but he never did. He kept promising but never showed up. Unfortunately, he had already been paid. Dad ended up having to take him to court. He got back some of the money but the rest we never saw again, in spite of a judgment against Jay. We later were told that the man had cancer and was very ill.

I found another contractor, who finished the upstairs. We had now paid three times what was initially projected for the renovations. We also had three renters. I moved from one apartment to another as they became finished and livable. After listing the property with the off-campus student housing office at the University, we received calls daily and developed a waiting list of possible renters.

We also unwittingly became figures in a local controversy involving the restoration of old buildings in the area.

Chapter 17

Life Goes On

Rocky Top you'll always be
Home sweet home to me
Good ol' Rocky Top
Rocky Top Tennessee,
Rocky Top Tennessee

- Official Tennessee state song

The Fort Sanders area in Knoxville was rich in history besides being right next to the university. During the late 1990s, much was made of the fact that so many of the elegant old homes and structures from the past had been torn down or were being allowed to fall down.

Some were being remodeled in atrocious architectural configurations, far from the character of the original structure and even farther from the original flavor of the neighborhood. This became a huge local issue and our student renters, who dearly loved our restored gray elephant, came down squarely on the side of saving history.

Dad, the reluctant landlord, was championed for his efforts to beautify, restore and ultimately save the Highland Avenue house, becoming an unlikely hero through no real effort of his own. He didn't care one way or the other about historical architecture. As far as he was concerned, he was just helping his daughter and really wanted no part of the whole thing.

After unintentionally being cast in this very noble role, however, he really took to heart the responsibility of being a landlord, going far beyond the call of duty. He and Mom took several of our tenants under their wing, treating them as family and staying in touch with them. If he could have, Dad would have let them live there for free.

While living at the Highland Avenue house, I also made a little money by parking cars in the yard during football season.

Parking, always a problem around campus, was even more intense when there was a University of Tennessee home football game.

Tennessee Volunteer fans take their football very seriously and are willing to pay premium prices to park and tailgate at home games. For hours prior to kickoff, the streets of Knoxville become a sea of orange and white, the university's colors, and Neyland Stadium becomes one of the largest cities in the state. Anyone who owned property around the area was out with signs, flags and lawn chairs three hours before any home game. You charged whatever your neighbors charged and directed cars toward a parking spot on your property, collecting cash as you went.

The first time, with Mom and Dad visiting me, I stood by the street in the alley flagging down folks and sent them to "Papa," who stood at the edge of the back yard, directing them where to park with a long, white stick. The next game I had repeat customers who asked where "Papa" was. But he was back in Wisconsin by then, missing the excitement.

Sports rivalry was particularly intense between the University of Tennessee and Florida. In 1998, The Vols were undefeated and playing against Florida at home. The competition was stiff, and UT won by only a field goal with about two seconds left on the overtime clock.

As usual, near the end of the night I could hear the crowd and horns and music coming from the direction of the stadium. I never needed to ask or watch the game to know who won. Louder than usual that night, our tenants were out in the yard jumping up and down. Neighbors and others were dancing in the street. The entire university area and adjacent neighborhood was then blocked off, forming a huge street party, and people were going wild.

The stadium crowd tore down a goal post en masse, and I heard they brought part of it to the firehouse one block from me. Once there, I'm told, it was sawed into tiny pieces to be shared by many. I thought it an interesting souvenir from an evening that would go down in the history of college football.

Our football parkers were always wonderful – good-natured, friendly and sometimes a little tipsy. One night a guy gave me forty bucks to let him stay in his car and sleep in our yard all night! Everyone was always in a good mood, at least before the games. I dressed in orange and white, too, and one time even dressed my cat Toby in a little orange and white cat T-shirt with the university logo. People came back looking for him next time, too.

The "TV set incident" lawsuit was settled out of court after four years in 1997. I had become desperate and impatient and my attorneys apparently knew nothing about TBI.

After the doctors and lawyers were paid, I ended up with a little over $40,000, which I immediately signed over to Dad – a partial payment toward the house. The agreement was that I would eventually buy it from him when I was able. The only problem was, he kept doing more to it, running up the cost so I had little hope of ever catching up enough to buy it. But that house with its big porch and dogwood tree in the back yard gave me sorely needed stability and a sense of security.

What bothered me the most about the whole "TV set incident" was that I lost something besides a contact lens and my dignity on the floor that night – I'd lost a big part of me. But I was beginning to get it back.

I graduated with a master's degree from the University of Tennessee in 1998.

Mom and Dad again came down for what they thought was my graduation, but it turned out to be a surprise party for their 50th wedding anniversary.

In preparation, Clark and I made numerous secret telephone calls to each other, getting names and addresses from Mom's address book and inviting everyone we knew – and some we didn't know.

On the day of the festivities, Mom, Dad and I had all gone to the huge arena where graduation was to be held, splitting up to go to our respective seats. I was to be on the floor level with Mom and Dad in the nosebleed section.

Knowing that all of us with mortarboards on the tops of our heads looked like ants from my parents' viewpoint and that they wouldn't be able to tell one from the other at that distance, I unobtrusively got up and left before the commencement ceremony even began.

Our house was so conveniently located to campus that the university van stopped at our door. I caught the van and went home, with Mom and Dad still sitting in the audience of the crowded arena, dutifully thinking they were watching their daughter get a diploma.

In the meantime, Clark and other family members had arrived and were putting up decorations, arranging furniture and greeting other guests. Aunt Evelyn was putting the finishing touches on an anniversary cake made to look like my parents wedding cake, based on 50-year old pictures.

A banner was hung across the front of the house. I was able to help make these last-minute preparations, then catch the van back to graduation again before the ceremony ended.

Meeting Mom and Dad outside the arena afterward, where they thought I had been all along, we headed home where Clark, Brian and the rest of the crowd were waiting.

My parents were none the wiser and truly surprised when friends and relatives from Wisconsin, Tennessee, Arizona, Florida and no telling where else appeared on our front porch. Clark and I were thrilled and I think everyone had a good time except for the stifling heat. We didn't have air conditioning in the house yet.

During this time I had seen little of Blondie, who still lived in Lenoir City. There were occasional telephone calls, and once she and a date came out to a club where I was selling roses and sitting in with the band. We still loved each other as family but had grown in different directions with a few miles between us.

I missed this tough-talking, brash, veteran truck-stop waitress. She had filled that vulnerable place in my heart that craved sisterhood. One day, I got a call from her.

"Watcha doin?" she cackled in her rowdy, husky voice.

"Laundry – what are *you* doing?" I asked. She was her usual wise-cracking, spirited self until her voice cracked and I asked her what was wrong.

"I…I had to go to the doctor. I've been having some tests and… some problems." She was at the hospital one block away from me.

"Carla," she whispered, "I have cancer in my brain..." I sat down.

She was still trying to sound tough, but I could tell she was crying. Many times married and having gone through yet another heartbreaking divorce, she was concerned about her young son.

"What will happen to Avery?" she sobbed.

"Just stay right there, I'll be there in just a minute," I told her. I ran to the hospital and found her within minutes, sitting alone in a waiting room.

Hugging her tightly, I asked what was going on. Her words and concerns came tumbling out on top of each other between tears: she was to undergo surgery and treatments, she had no money, what would happen to her son, and on and on. Mostly I just listened, asking about second opinions, options, helping her calm down and make a plan.

Finally, I told her she needed to be brave, and upon leaving I pressed something into her hand that I had impulsively grabbed as I was leaving the house: Lynn's Purple Heart Medal. He had devalued his numerous military awards, but as she opened her hand to look at it, her expression instantly turned to one of determination, resolve and gratitude. But after a brave and lengthy battle, she died Aug. 29, 1999, and lies next to Lynn and their father.

Getting my master's degree had whet my appetite for learning once again, and I continued to take classes. School gave me a sense of direction, purpose and accomplishment. By doing the rose route regularly, I was almost able to catch up on bills and stay afloat financially. In all this time, I had received almost nothing from Dave as far as child support.

Brian had met a young woman from Memphis who was attending the University of Tennessee. They became a steady item, and he eventually moved to Memphis with her, where he stayed for the next eight years.

I began dating again sporadically. There was Michael, the Chicago-style gangster who was apparently hiding from the law by staying with his sister in rural Kentucky, and Pete, the real estate hustler who wanted to help me sell my house. There was John, the handyman, Ed, a genuine Philadelphia lawyer, and Don, the accountant. He lasted the longest.

Together, Don and I visited Charleston, S.C., where he had attended college and I spent many hours at his country home. But he didn't think I was "country" enough for his taste and he was probably right. The last I heard, he was involved with a woman who butchered her own hogs.

Some gentlemen seemed to have the delusion that I had money. They may have heard of the lawsuit and labored under the misconception that I had sued for millions. While it's true that I would have given all for love and was generous with what I had, I didn't really have much to give and was still hurting financially.

One relationship got as far as taking the young man home for Christmas and introducing him to my family before I found out he was seeing another woman. I made friends with his girlfriend, who confirmed my worst fears, before retreating to another mind-numbing but temporary depression.

I swore off any future romantic entanglements.

I also acquired a new family during this time, largely responsible for giving my life more meaning and structure.

❧

Victoria had been a high-ranking executive with a major organization in East Tennessee but had become a victim of downsizing. Her husband was out of work at the same time, so she eventually took a position as a consultant, requiring her to travel to another state for several days out of the week. Her husband then joined a firm out of state as well, leaving a gap in child care for their three adolescent children. After a succession of young ladies from the university filled the role, I applied for the job.

Alas, I was not Mary Poppins.

As a nanny, my cooking lacked in originality and finesse, my homework skills were not quite up to par and my organizational skills not what they used to be, but I was able to feel love for these children and perhaps that was what counted most. In spite of my ongoing memory problems, I could also remember what it was like to be a child. And although a far cry from their cool, hip, young caretakers of the past, I had experienced motherhood, weathered a few crises in my life and had developed a lot of patience. I proved to be utterly unflappable, a valuable quality given the number of crises, last minute projects, and split-second decisions to be made. I had minored in child development at the University of Utah and now remembered certain tricks and techniques, but my love for these children came naturally.

Staying at their big house in a tree-lined neighborhood four days a week, I became their second mom. I attended meetings at school, fed the cat and took them to Boy Scout meetings and piano lessons. I got to know their friends, tastes and habits. I alternately nagged and praised, like a mother.

It felt a little strange when Victoria came home on Thursdays, because even though I had been on a similar career track, I was now content to be a stay-at -home mom for her children.

❧

Although I had made peace with myself while doing the rose route, there was always a feeling that some vital part of me was missing.

The head injury, I had come to feel, had robbed me of my personality, made up of memories, opinions, attitudes, experiences, knowledge, likes and dislikes. I'd experienced none of the above for a while. There was simply no depth of emotion, few complex functional cognitive processes and not much memory, but now, very gradually, I was beginning to feel whole again.

Over time, I had created new memories without even realizing it, where once there had been a vacuum. A semblance of stability was achieved, which allowed me to relax somewhat. Developing a relationship with the children, not worrying so much about finances, and my academic victories all helped me to heal.

For a while I had looked for success and found only failure. It had stopped me in my tracks. What I didn't realize, however, was that in failure I still gained a new experience to catalog. It was progress. I was no longer a blank slate.

A pinball careens around the machine bouncing from side to side. In doing so, it is subtly, eventually directed to a route that will accomplish some objective.

With some machines there may be several routes, or several objectives, each counting for so many points, but the ball must be set in motion first. I now consciously set myself in motion, allowing myself to bounce from side to side while looking for alternate routes and objectives. Perhaps there was something to be gained in just trying.

Hence, the rebuilding of my personality began.

Chapter 18

Metamorphosis

He's a pinball wizard,
There has to be a twist.
A pinball wizard,
Got such a supple wrist!

- Pinball Wizard, The Who

I decided to actively keep trying new experiences and still looked for things that I was good at or at least liked. I also told myself I would not dismiss the things I previously disliked or found I was not good at. A personality is shaped by both positive and negative experiences, therefore, I determined that every experience had value.

I would rejoice at any successes, no matter how small, I would also allow myself to fail, realizing that it wouldn't be the end of the world. Maybe I wasn't a great keyboard player any more, so what? What else could I be or do? It was time to explore. In order to do this, I had to consciously let go of the old me.

Although it sounds melodramatic and tragic, I had to accept the idea that the old me had "died"- and it truly felt like a death.

When I mentioned this to Dr. Chironna, he concurred. Instead of depressing me, his casual, honest agreement lent validity to my feelings.

Like Tom Sawyer listening to his own funeral in Aunt Polly's parlor, I observed my own demise, a death of the spirit, intellect and emotions. Only by facing this reality was I eventually able to accept it. Through acceptance, I was able to begin the mourning process and grieve. Only then was I free to move on.

When a death occurs, the realization that the departed isn't coming back comes at some point. You slowly begin to pick up the pieces and prepare to build a new life.

I acknowledged to myself that it was time to forge ahead. I began thinking in terms of opportunities to develop aspects of what I now thought of as the new me.

The living shell still existed, and I needed to fill it with something. It felt like a gradual rebirth in which I now played an active role. I wondered if a caterpillar was aware that it was becoming a butterfly during the metamorphosis process?

I began consistently using just my initials instead of my full given name. I didn't realize it at the time, but this may have been a subconscious effort to establish this new personality.

For the first time in several years, I began to feel like something besides a spectator in my own life. I began to accept responsibility for who I was, my own shortcomings, my weaknesses and eventually, my strengths. In becoming an active participant, I also began to find courage.

Around this time, I finally began seeing a slightly older gentleman from Lake City.

Johnny had followed me from club to club, bought entire baskets of flowers and was extremely persistent. He had been in sales, had his own beautiful home overlooking vast acreage, had grown children and was recently divorced. A stocky fellow with almost white hair, he was gruff and blustery and had a twinkle in his eye that brought Santa Claus to mind.

I knew his type: lonely, depressed, drinking too much, mistrustful of women and aging faster than he would like. He saw something in me that seemed to calm and reassure him. He showed up every place I sold roses.

Eventually I came to think of him as a friend. Still, he really was not my type. Having been through numerous dating disasters and bad relationships, I had learned not to trust men and wasn't looking for romance. In fact, I was actually trying to avoid it.

It is precisely this quality which made the chase even more enjoyable for my new friend.

He spoke of certain values and came across as a fairly decent sort of fellow. He was funny, patient and kind with me.

Finally, I gave him my phone number. However, still jaded and not really interested, I told him jokes whenever he called, hoping to avoid any real conversations about relationships, dating or furthering our friendship.

After months of phone calls, jokes, an occasional turn on the dance floor and a late night dinner or two at the Waffle House after my rose route, I finally took pity on him. I thought, why not give him an honest chance to win my affections? He couldn't do anything worse to me than a half-dozen or more so-called boyfriends had already done. Besides, he had known me long enough to realize that I was not a party girl, a drunk, an opportunist, a dumb-ass or dishonest. Maybe I was what he was looking for in a woman, as he kept telling me. Could he be what I wanted in a man?

Maybe this one man could see beyond the packaging and appreciate the real me. Perhaps I had given up on men too soon.

We now spent hours on the phone, discussing everything from our families to religion, and within two months he excitedly declared me to be the perfect woman for him. Knowing him to be on the rebound, I backed off slightly, alarmed by his desire to jump in headfirst. Lasting relationships, I now knew, needed time to grow and the best seemed to be built on trust, respect and friendship. I'd had enough relationships for all the wrong reasons with all the wrong men. I wanted to do it right this time, if I was going to do it at all.

I soon found myself on the back of his motorcycle, following him around the grocery store or helping in his garden. I met his children, friends and even his ex-wife. He met my parents and my son.

I spent more and more time at his house and came to think of it as home. We adopted a pet goose, rode around looking for deer in the countryside and sang songs in the car. We visited his family cemetery, I played the little organ at his house and sang hymns on Sunday. I loved the smell of wood in his shop. One year he labored for weeks making me a custom-designed table for Christmas.

When he went on a special hunting trip with his buddies, I secretly tucked little notes and treats in his belongings while helping him pack, and he called daily from South Dakota. I decorated his huge rustic living room for Christmas and gradually began to feel like the lady of the house although I still had my own home in Knoxville.

We brought out the best in each other. My easygoing nature and naturally sunny disposition seemed to complement his excitable, temperamental side. His curious native intelligence complemented my years of formal education. I enjoyed talking about business with him and was amused at some of his political opinions and his spontaneous streak of mischief.

Eventually, I fell for this vulnerable, generous soul. Gradually we both learned to trust again and would have trusted each other with our lives.

My income was enough to live on, but I couldn't save anything or buy any big-ticket items.

The world was fast becoming computerized, and I had a taste of it on campus. In the computer lab, I had discovered that I could now type in my own unique hunt-and-peck style faster that I could write, thereby capturing the flyaway thoughts that so often escaped my overtaxed brain. I also found help with my spelling problems in spell check. However, I didn't know much about computers and became lost and confused in computer classes.

I decided the best thing would be for me to get one of my own and play around with it at my own pace, in my spare time.

Johnny loaned me the money to buy a used computer, monitor and printer. I was able to pay him back very shortly and became comfortable with this old computer, teaching myself the basics.

Then he loaned me the money to have laser surgery on my eyes. He had gotten tired of me fussing with my contact lenses in the evening while he waited to cuddle. I had been following the progress of corrective eye surgery ever since I'd first heard of experimental radial keratotomy surgeries in Russia while still in junior high school. I had kept abreast because those coke bottle-bottom eyeglasses had been the bane of my existence for years, and contact lenses, although I was very grateful for them, were a nuisance.

I had been teased mercilessly, not only about my vision but also because of my hearing deficit and more.

My teeth and hair, both now bleached, my weight under control and my eyes finally free from the shielding spectacles added up to a drastic improvement in my appearance, even without the wigs and flashy clothes. I was gaining more self-esteem from the inside out. Johnny's love helped. He was very much a part of me, and I was making positive progress in life.

I might always have the hearing problem and my brain may never be the same, but I was determined to work with what I had and find ways around obstacles.

I took a course specifically on Traumatic Brain Injury at the University of Tennessee where I became the class case study. I was a member of a panel on brain injury at the State TBI Convention and on campus. I wrote an article for the campus newspaper during Brain Injury Awareness week.

Writing, I now discovered, was a great outlet for me. I wrote and sold several articles to magazines during this time. Sometimes I still had trouble speaking, especially in strange or tense situations, but I could spend hours writing.

I also found that I really enjoyed certain types of research and where I had been quite detail-oriented before, I now grasped the big picture easily. I was able to maintain almost complete objectivity in most situations.

On certain tests I didn't do very well, with some cognitive processes impaired because of a dyslexic-type disorder, but I scored off the charts in creativity and intuitiveness.

I learned to use a tiny tape recorder to make notes to myself, developed the habit of making lists, simplified financial matters with direct deposit and debit whenever possible, and learned to control stress.

The medical community had been wrong about the brain regenerating within two years *if it was going to.* Over the years I had felt myself learning, grasping, changing and eventually even felt a great deal like the old me, whom I at one time thought dead. This new me was even better in some ways. This new version was, if possible, even more spontaneous and flexible than the old me. The new me began to grasp certain concepts faster than the old me and could cut through to the heart of the matter quickly.

Some people have trouble dealing squarely with reality. Either they can't see it or won't accept it. The head injury seemed to make it so I could deal *only* with reality.

This was what I wanted my relationship with Johnny to be based on, not thrills, notions of romance or games. I wanted substance this time, something lasting and beautiful. Something real.

All of us bear scars from past wounds, both mental and physical. The psychological baggage I had carried before seemed to have been knocked out of me with the head injury, and I hadn't added it to the rebuilding process.

I had a newfound spirituality and a personal closeness with the Creator now that was with me always. There was a gradual, simple, honest and profound faith in a Holy Spirit, a higher being, a God.

Where I once felt I couldn't trust anyone, I now had complete and absolute, almost childlike trust in this higher power.

My newfound faith did not come through Scriptures, study, missionary work or church attendance. I'm not sure I even know myself how it came to be, but it's still there, ingrained in the very core of my being, unquestioning and unyielding. It is a very private thing that gives me strength, wisdom, guidance and joy. I forgive and love easily. It directs my every thought and action without my even having to think about it. It evokes a certain gratitude that guides my moods and allows me to live in the moment as well as feeling grounded in the future.

I've learned to take each day at a time and survive.

By now, I was much more patient and less stressed. I came to feel that whatever was meant to be would be, and I was all right with that. It's possible that because I had already been through so much, I figured that whatever happened to me couldn't be any worse than what I'd already been through.

My time at Johnny's was stress-free and peaceful. It allowed me to heal at my own pace. I was able to find pleasure in the simple things in life in a very supportive environment.

I've heard it said that being happy doesn't mean everything's perfect; it just means you've decided to see beyond the imperfections. I had walked a million miles in baby steps toward recovery from the brain injury and was learning to see beyond my own imperfections. I was happy.

Johnny became my strength and security, but I wasn't exactly sure what I was to him. I knew he loved me, but also knew that this kind of love was a horse of a different color for both of us. Neither of us ever had any experience with a serious relationship based upon mutual respect, shared values and integrity.

Neither of us particularly wanted to marry again. He, out of fear, having already been though two disastrous and financially draining marriages; and in my case, because I would lose my VA health insurance, especially necessary for anyone with a pre-existing condition.

While we didn't discuss marriage, Johnny, a rather traditional man with some old world values, didn't want to "live in sin" either. His frail, elderly mother was still alive, and he respected her and his upbringing enough to want to do right in her eyes, the eyes of his family and in his own eyes.

We were both happy and I felt more loved and stable than I ever had before, but as several years passed, I began to feel on edge. I also felt the need for some kind of acknowledgement, commitment and more security.

Were we just going to coast forever? Was there a future here? How long could I continue to live in two places? I was still taking care of Victoria's children as well.

Never taking anything for granted, I wasn't sure that the bubble of happiness wouldn't burst someday and Johnny wouldn't turn on me at some point, yet I wasn't exactly sure what I wanted from this man or what I was willing to give.

We had never been angry with each other and never had a fight. We agreed to disagree on some things but still valued each other's opinions.

Nothing was *wrong* with us, but I began to feel like I was shouldering most of the emotional responsibility.

I knew that I could have used my womanly wiles on him and manipulated him from the start, but I wanted him to take some responsibility.

Above all, I wanted an honest relationship. I wanted him to be with me because he genuinely wanted to be there, not because I had played any games with him. I didn't do all that I could have done to keep his interest alive or fan the smoldering flames of passion.

Because I didn't want to play games and because of our lack of direction, I began to lose some confidence in the relationship. With no plans for a future together, I was beginning to feel slightly off-guard, like I was drifting aimlessly. I gradually stopped taking much of an interest in his place and began paying more attention to my little apartment on Highland.

That spirit of restlessness was back.

Victoria's consulting job was playing out, and the children were almost able to care for themselves. My position at their house was now largely that of chauffeur. They had gotten a new dog, to which I was highly allergic, and I made plans to leave my new family. I was very proud of "my" kids and felt that I had been a positive influence in their lives.

Wanting more from my own life now, I knew that any new job would have to allow me flexibility and a certain freedom to navigate my own course because of my limitations. I combed the want ads and Internet in Knoxville and elsewhere.

I found old letters of recommendation and networked. I also presented my model for program development, a class assignment, at the National Indian Education Association Convention in Nashville where I saw my old friend Sky Blue.

A lot of the "old me" had returned. Once again, I enjoyed training and teaching. Presenting new ideas, facilitating the learning process and encouraging creative thought were exciting to me. Seeing the light of discovery in a student's eyes was thrilling. My biggest reward was sharing their ensuing enthusiasm.

I took freelance training jobs and temporary assignments. I coached classmates, who by now were coming to me in search of ideas for class presentations. I found simple software that could help me write customized policies and procedures and offered this to previous contacts.

Promoting some of the personal development and extra mile training material from so long ago in Salt Lake City, I was able to customize presentations to the needs of primarily small to mid-sized organizations and businesses who couldn't afford a full-time trainer.

Gradually, while job-hunting, business began coming to me. I became so busy that I had to utilize classmates for some jobs. What money I made, I put back into the business.

Once in a conference room, I was pitching a three-part training series to a health care facility. The atmosphere was plush but sterile and bland. Everyone wore suits, including me, and all were equipped for note taking. They were quiet, expectant and ready to either challenge or be bored.

One looked at his watch, another set up her laptop computer. My audience was intelligent and educated, immaculately groomed, impeccably-dressed and well-mannered but a little stiff. I thought they might be out of touch with "the common folk" and I attempted to put them in touch by initiating a role playing exercise.

My theater background came to the rescue as they slowly came alive.

Involved now and seeing my point, they finally *got it.* Laughter, followed by discussion. Another exercise. More laughter. I'm on a roll. We bonded. We discussed employee motivation and the role it plays in learning. We discussed being part of a team. We discussed leadership.

Excellent dialog, I thought to myself as I headed to my car.

Stopping momentarily in my tracks, I realized this was the first time I truly felt I was back in the saddle again, on a professional level. I wanted to get down on my knees and weep tears of joy, feeling like another part of the old me had indeed returned. Silently, gratefully, I acknowledged my thanks to the Creator.

The old talent for reading an audience was coming back. Perhaps another part of the old me that instinctively knew how to present information was back, but very quickly I realized there were major differences.

With an enhanced spiritual awareness combined with some new skills for seeing the big picture and cutting to the chase, I was able to make quicker assessments of problems, make recommendations and serve as a consultant for several businesses.

I was able to branch out in new directions. I felt that I had been guided through the eye of a storm by God himself. Like many who have been given a second chance, I wanted to make the most of it. My career was my avenue to better things.

I tried to incorporate a certain creativity and flair into even the most mundane presentations and events and never forgot my lessons concerning motivation and enthusiasm learned at Tellico and in Salt Lake City. Again utilizing my improvisational theater training, I incorporated role-playing and games often into sometimes complicated, sometimes hilarious meetings.

In a teambuilding exercise, for instance, we played *Gilligan's Island,* based on an old sitcom from the 1960s.

The basic premise of the show was; a small group of people have become shipwrecked on a deserted island. Week after week, they hatched elaborate plans to get back to civilization, only to repeatedly fail in their attempts.

My participants actually got off the island during class and took it a step further. With taxes, traffic and bureaucracy on the mainland, they decided they liked it better on the island, so devised a plan to go back. To heck with civilisation!

My workshops were fun, exciting and beneficial. People who laugh together and share common experiences bond easily. I kept expanding with each new idea and found willing takers through previous contacts.

My philosophy was that learning could be - and should be - fun.

I was still seeing Johnny. We discussed the possibilities in the trucking industry, with which we were both very familiar.

While pursuing this, I gradually realized that my business was getting bigger than I ever intended. If this kept up, I would have to actually hire people, get an accountant, a business manager and begin marketing in earnest.

I stayed busy, but I was not driven, nor did I want to become so busy that I would have no time to stop and smell the roses. I still smelled them in my car, doing the rose route on weekends, when I wasn't doing anything else.

Deciding I was ready for a *real* job with insurance, a 401K and a corporate structure, I sold my fledgling business and began the search for employment in earnest.

Gradually cutting back on my other activities, I was now dedicated to finding the perfect job for me. Thinking myself ready to relocate if necessary, I was also ready to sell my beloved house.

I tried not to think about what might happen between Johnny and me because although there was love, there was no commitment on either of our parts.

In the fall of 2001, I found the job…and sold the house.

Part 4
Nashville

Chapter 19

Nashville cats and new challenges

One of these days I'm gonna settle down
And take you back with me to the Guitar Town

- Guitar Town, Steve Earle

Even while selling roses in East Tennessee, I would occasionally drive the three hours and end up at Tootsies Orchid Lounge, a mainstay of Nashville's country night life, spending the rest of the week with my cousin Lois.

Long ago I had felt intimidated and disillusioned when in Nashville, but in later years while visiting I became accustomed to its unique spirit and character. I now felt at home playing music on Broadway and in the honky-tonks, going backstage at the Grand Ole Opry and at writer's nights. I connected with musicians and writers at every opportunity.

Songwriter Matraca Berg writes that "dreams die hard around here," and indeed everyone carried their own piece of a dream as they waited tables, played for tips and wrote lyrics on napkins and food wrappers.

I was at Wolfy's when Merle Haggard dropped by to sit in with the band and I was at the Stockyards Lounge when Johnny Paycheck jammed with the house band during the Country Music Association's Fan Fair. I did literally run into Alan Jackson on the street and Wynonna

Judd at a local department store. Through Lois, I was privy to the inside gossip of this entertainment-oriented tourist mecca.

I'd had the opportunity to meet some country music giants and rub elbows with legends, but I was in awe of only one - the late Porter Wagoner, long time host of the Grand Ole Opry and Dolly Parton's early mentor.

My longstanding infatuation with this country gentleman, known for his splashy, sparkling stage attire and heartfelt, homespun music, was a point of hilarity among my fellow musicians, since I was generally unimpressed with stardom and had a bit of a reputation as more of a rocker.

When I finally got to meet him, I fell to his feet, begging to touch "just one rhinestone." Others in the room were laughing (and he seemed amused as well) while I threatened to cling to his leg as he left the dressing room. Later, I mourned his death on a very personal level.

I threatened to mug Little Jimmy Dickens, another Grand Ole Opry regular, in the parking lot and steal his sequin-encrusted suit, but he didn't appear afraid of me. His large sense of humor and good nature more than made up for his small stature.

I encountered the great writer Harlan Howard and the incomparable George Jones in a restaurant and Billy Ray Cyrus at a music store.

Lois had some powerful and influential friends in the music business with whom we often socialized. When one of them died, we went to the funeral. Like a scene out of a movie, in the drizzling rain the black limousines and umbrellas surrounded the Catholic church where the eulogy was offered. Country music icons Willie Nelson and Connie Smith sang.

The rain accompanied me after midnight as I walked through downtown Nashville, from one honky-tonk to another, with their interchangeable and ever-hopeful artists in residence, my friends.

But I had a day job now.

As program coordinator for a new joint program of United Auto Workers and Ford Motor Company in Nashville, I would be developing educational, recreational and volunteer opportunities and activities for employees, retirees, their families and the community.

My father was a long-time Teamster and union supporter, so I was proud to be entering his world in this way. Thus, I moved to Nashville not to be in the music business but as a contract employee of Ford Motor Company and United Auto Workers.

The new program was essentially a work in progress, so I would be in on the ground floor like at Tellico. We would be building a center dedicated to education, families and communities, all values of which I held dear.

The Americans with Disabilities Act requires employers to make accommodations for handicapped workers, but I mentioned only the hearing impairment during my original interview, mindful of a stigma associated with disorders of the brain.

I had already noticed that when people knew about the brain injury, they sometimes scrutinized me more closely and expectations may have been altered. Perhaps subconsciously, people seemed to expect either more or less of me than what I could deliver. I also felt that the injury hadn't been an impairment in anything I had done lately.

In truth, I didn't know what modifications could be made to accommodate this particular disability because it wasn't as simple as installing a ramp or telephone system for the deaf.

Although I had recovered a great deal and learned my way around obstacles, the nature and degree of the handicap seemed ever-changing. Of course, there were still many things I hadn't tried yet.

I did state that I needed some autonomy and flexibility in my work environment and schedule so I could attend doctor appointments and the like. I was thrilled when offered the job.

Johnny was very supportive, as he had been of all of my endeavors. I had mixed emotions about that. Part of me wanted him to say, "Please don't go. Just find something you like around here, let's be together forever, we'll make it!"

He might have felt it but he didn't say it. He may also have felt that he hadn't much to offer me after his two divorces or that he didn't want to hold me back. Through tears, in private, I decided perhaps he really didn't want me at all. Did I still want him?

I went to his house alone one afternoon and said farewell to the only place where I had ever really felt the happiness and comfort of having a helpmate.

Saying goodbye to the dogs, I realized my heart would always be in this particular spot in East Tennessee, and probably part of my heart would always be with this man.

Then I proceeded with plans to leave. I *was* excited about the job.

Johnny helped me move to Nashville and we were both prepared for the relationship to end, or so we thought. When he drove away, my heart ached as I thought of him not being a part of my life, but what was done was done. Ours had been a warm, loving, grounded and stable relationship. We were good for each other and good to each other, but there was no commitment whatsoever.

I've heard that some people come into our lives for a reason, a season or a lifetime. Perhaps some relationships were meant to be temporary and maybe Johnny and I were there for each other at a time when we both needed someone. Maybe that was our reason for being together. But I thought we were both ready to let go and move on.

In Nashville, Lois and I became temporary roommates. I was once again reunited with my friend Rick from my theater days of long ago and returned to Chaffin's Barn Dinner Theatre as a guest. Everything looked the same as I remembered and I began learning my way around my new town in earnest, other than the honky-tonks and the Opry.

Much to my surprise, Johnny began calling immediately - and I called him. We spoke daily, if not more often. I had the feeling he missed me much more than he let on. It seemed that we were still in a relationship, albeit a long-distance one. I made plans to go back to his place on weekends, but usually these fell through.

Learning my new job took a tremendous amount of time, and I stayed exhausted. Now I was the one who couldn't see a future with Johnny and felt that being an absentee significant other was unfair to him. His calls made my day, but I told him if he wanted to, he could date others, hoping in my heart that he wouldn't want to. He continued to call.

For months the bond stayed intact. Through time and distance I knew what he was doing, when he would call and when he was doing something he shouldn't, just as I had with Lynn. He was still my rock, my world and more, through the difficult first days of a new job, yet another ear surgery and my other activities. I came to rely on these phone calls.

They became my lifeline, and his voice at the other end of the wire was my salvation.

❧

I loved my job, but although I initially saw my boss as a friend and there were many similarities in our lives, the differences were significant.

She had been in a relatively stable position for 10 years. I had jumped around a lot. She had her own way of doing things that didn't quite gel with the approach I was accustomed to from other businesses and my graduate classes. She had come from a nonprofit background, I had come from the crass world of commercialism and show business. I was flashy, she was conservative. Also, I may have been too eager and more excited than she knew about having a real job again. My enthusiasm may have frightened her.

I had long ago learned to adapt information and process it through channels that worked for me, but my boss wasn't quite comfortable with anyone who didn't work exactly the same way she did. For instance, she favored spreadsheets with grids: Excel boxes of information. The way my still easily confused brain functioned, the grids were only extra visual distractions.

I did better with just straight lists, but during a meeting one day, she became agitated that I wasn't looking at the spreadsheet she thought I should be looking at, not knowing that I usually redid them later in a form with which I was more comfortable.

I actually avoided spreadsheets.

I had learned to take notes on everything because I still lacked confidence in my memory, and I always checked them before I spoke. Better to be safe than sorry, I thought. This may have translated to her as not being quite on top of things.

Because I was now a major multi-tasker, my mind may have been on several things at once or a month or two into the future, while my hands were busy with today. I was also comfortable with a certain degree of improvisation and spontaneity, probably a holdover from show biz. I now imagine this would have felt, to her, like being totally out of control.

For a time, it was only the two of us. I was pressing for results, thinking ahead, trying to keep up with corporate changes, which sometimes came daily, and tending to the details involved in quality programming. We were still experimenting.

Often my supervisor and I were not on the same page. I had the feeling that because she was being micro-managed by the home office, she thought she needed to micro-manage me. My free-wheeling, easier-to-get-forgiveness-than-permission (within reason) style was at odds with what I saw as her by-the-book rigidity.

Success is a funny thing. Much of the time, no one cares how it is achieved. It can be bought, stolen, invented, borrowed or worked for, but once achieved, everyone wants part of it, and it paves the way for more success. Sometimes getting there involves risk.

Some people like to be safe and stick with the tried and true. They don't like making waves, being at the forefront or on the cutting edge. To them, mediocrity means safety. Others thrive on navigating uncharted territory, creativity and trying new things.

There is a direct, documented correlation between calculated risk and success, between innovation and leadership.

I was a risk-taker. My goal in any situation was to be the best. To me, achieving that translated into some degree of job security, references, recommendations and more opportunities. I had learned from experience that being the best often involved being unique and original, and in the end, I knew that no one would argue with success, as far as our program or anything else.

I could be unique and original, and I also utilized my talent, developed early, for reading an audience. This was just a different setting. I had come to rely on this, as well as my intuition.

I felt that I knew what needed to happen to make our programs successful, although we were still in uncharted territory. I had known it would be challenging. It was made even more challenging by my relationship with my supervisor. At odds with each other for months, I sometimes felt that I couldn't do anything right. I later came to feel she simply didn't like me - a classic personality conflict. Many times she was short with me and I wanted to quit.

I had been told that I was hired for my creativity and resourcefulness but constantly felt muzzled or ignored. Well, I could adjust. I had a lot to offer. I was, however, beginning to experience some setbacks. With my confidence flagging, my speech problems began to recur. When my boss asked me a question, I sometimes stuttered and was extremely uncomfortable around her. I began to shy away from addressing groups and found myself withdrawing slightly.

When a co-worker was hired, I was initially glad to have someone to share the work load, but before long, she showed herself to be mean-spirited and ill-tempered. Her mood swings were unexpected and intense, and she seemed to have a need to be the teacher's pet, ingratiating herself with our supervisor.

In all fairness, although I was slightly shocked by her temperamental outbursts, she was a single mother, still quite young herself and probably totally stressed out. I bit my tongue, went about my business and hoped she would eventually chill out a bit.

I didn't want to just do my job. Accustomed to assuming an active leadership role, I wanted our center to be No. 1 - the best in the country. It was a daunting task, but I was up for it.

To promote our programs within the workplace and in the community, we called upon celebrities. Jack Greene from the Grand Ole Opry, singer Brenda Lee and several local celebrities were kind enough to pay us a visit. I made business contacts on behalf of the organization and planned large-scale events.

The people we served became my friends. Indeed, the employees and retirees of the industrial plant we served were an incredible group of people: hard-working, conscientious and loyal. I found in them the lasting friendship and respect I didn't get from my two co-workers. Drawing solace and strength through them, I focused on the task at hand.

I developed programs, ideas and activities, forged partnerships and constantly sought new ideas. Some of the events I coordinated, including an annual Veteran's Day program, enjoyed phenomenal success. I think that was why I was not fired outright.

Still, in spite of my successes, it seemed that everything I did irritated my two colleagues, and things became worse. I would offer a suggestion or ask a question during a meeting, and it would be dismissed or not even acknowledged. I still thought about quitting and sometimes felt that I was being goaded into leaving. However, the reality was that in spite of the pettiness, lack of support and obvious disdain from my co-workers, I loved my job.

Chapter 20

Four-footed friends

You know a dream is like a river
Ever changin' as it flows
And a dreamer's just a vessel
That must follow where it goes
Trying to learn from what's behind you
And never knowing what's in store
Makes each day a constant battle
Just to stay between the shores...

- The River, Garth Brooks

Brian was having his own problems in Memphis, and I was trying to help him. I was also worried about my dad's health. By then, he'd already had open-heart surgery back in Wisconsin.

I bought a condo when I first went to Nashville. Then I bought a duplex that needed refurbishing.

Lois became ill on several occasions, and I drove her to hospitals and doctor appointments.

I had a lot going on. There were days when things were so bad at work that I felt I had made the wrong decision in coming to Nashville and wished I were still selling roses back in East Tennessee.

There were, above all, many days when I ached to just see and hold my dear friend and companion, Johnny, but reminded myself that he could have stopped me from leaving if he'd really had any interest in doing so. Still, he was a constant presence in my life via the telephone.

I had even thought about working for a year then returning to the house on the hill and his loving arms. His calls remained my lifeline and an island of hope in a sea of frustration and worry during my early days with UAW-Ford until the day he simply called and ended it. Overnight. There was no explanation, no consolation, no warning. It was just over.

There was now no communication with him whatsoever. I wondered how he could be so cold. I tried to call him. Sometimes he sounded anguished and other times he would hang up on me. I wrote him several letters but received no response.

There had been nothing we couldn't talk about and I sought his advice as he sometimes sought mine. Now I had no one to talk to.

There had been a level of comfort between Johnny and me that I had never found in someone of the opposite sex. I had begun to truly feel that this bond would stretch into eternity, even if we hadn't seen each other for several months. I knew this man better than he knew himself most of the time.

He had always said he would value the friendship, but I knew friends didn't treat friends this way. I suspected he was seeing someone else but he should have told me.

The weeks turned into months. I dealt with it the best way I knew. I just stayed busy. I couldn't quit my job now, it was my therapy.

I worked long hours adding personal touches and sought outside resources, sometimes at my own expense. I was a dedicated overachiever who was now absolutely driven. In the past, I had been in the position where if something wasn't successful I didn't get paid and I was single-mindedly determined to make this a success.

Results-oriented by nature, I was in my element dreaming up ideas from projects to classes to skits to contests. I browsed the aisles of costumes, props, wigs and assorted mayhem at Performance Studios in downtown Nashville, getting ideas and stimulating my creativity. I networked within the community and facilitated workshops and classes. I arranged field trips, employee discounts and special events.

One of my projects was "Kids at College Day" where children of employees got to spend time on Tennessee State University campus. Faculty had designed special age-appropriate classes for them, and they even got to eat lunch with the college president.

It was a personal challenge to build this program, and I still loved my job in spite of the ongoing problems with my co-workers. But not one day went by that I didn't think of Johnny, and very few days passed that I didn't shed a tear for my long-lost pal.

People like Johnny sometimes subconsciously court danger, even in relationships. Perhaps he knew he was safe with me.

Sometimes, the worse people like Johnny are treated, the better they like it. Alas, I had treated him well.

His complete abandonment of even the friendship both puzzled and saddened me. But out of the ashes, I realized that perhaps I had lost nothing. I had gained from knowing him and healed at his hands. I knew in my heart that we had been together for all the right reasons.

Later, I found out that he was indeed trying to establish a relationship with a new girlfriend after giving up on our long-distance affair. Johnny, with his all-or-nothing thinking, couldn't be friends with an old girlfriend while trying to win over another. True friendship with a member of the opposite sex is not a concept that comes easily to an aging redneck.

As time went by, Johnny's new relationship didn't work out and we began seeing each other again. I went back to East Tennessee regularly on weekends now. We were still close, and he seemed to appreciate me more than ever, even buying me a car, but somehow, although I still felt love, I didn't feel quite the same.

In my absence, and in a misguided attempt to buy the heart of my replacement, he had acquired three new family members. These four-footed creatures resided in his barn and the fields surrounding his house.

Upon first seeing them, my heart sank, knowing I couldn't even be downwind of three horses because of my allergies. And I resented them too, having been originally intended as a gift to the brief interim sweetheart.

At first, I experienced a little minor wheezing and kept my distance. They were big, and I was afraid of them. I didn't go near Johnny if he had been near the animals, nor did I go near the saddles or other riding gear. I thought him crazy to have gotten them in the first place and didn't know what purpose they served. But whenever we came driving up the driveway, they would be there waiting to greet us. They stood still and patient, their big brown eyes taking in everything.

Tentatively, I occasionally stood closer and spoke to them. I noticed that I didn't get sick right away like I expected and attributed it to the wind blowing and being out in the open, up on the hill.

I watched as Johnny fed and led them around. It was as though they each had a distinct personality of their own and seemed to enjoy being around people.

One day, on a whim, I decided to feed them. I got a scoop of sweet feed and gingerly approached them. Then I got another scoop, and another.

The next day, I fed them again. They were close enough and I patted one on the nose, thinking I would immediately break out in a rash and have to be hospitalized. It was a chance I just had to take.

I knew I was flirting with disaster, but no rash appeared.

I began to feed them almost daily. I also began to pet them more and talk to them. They seemed to respond as I spoke.

Johnny just treated them like troublesome objects. I now held lengthy conversations with them, got on their side of the fence and did silly things with them. I whinnied, stomped my foot and threw my head back in the wind like they did.

I began reading about horses, their habits and the process of training them, becoming particularly interested in Monte Roberts, a modern-day horse whisperer, and his gentle training techniques. Not wanting them to think of me as their meal ticket, I let Johnny worry about feeding time.

I began going out into the field with them daily, eventually grooming them, I even tried to ride once or twice. When one gave birth to a colt, I felt like a proud grandmother.

Johnny might come home to find me sitting out in the field in the sun, singing to two sleeping horses, one with her big head in my lap, the other lying nearby.

"...and if that mockingbird don't sing, Mama's gonna buy you a diamond ring…," my voice fell softly across the meadow.

Their favorite song was *Red River Valley,* over and over and over. And over.

"...Just remember the Red River Valley and the cowboy who loved you so true…"

I believe they thought I was one of them, just with a slightly better singing voice.

Always careful, I used common sense around these majestic animals and began to train one of them by planting sugar cubes, apples and handfuls of favorite food throughout the fields. I would lead her with a rope to all the spots where they were hidden. She seemed to think I was very smart to know where all these hidden goodies were and acted as though she looked forward to walking with me, and I enjoyed it just as much.

After finding a pile of feed or several apples, her big brown eyes seemed to say, "That was good... Do you know where there's more?" and I would lead her to another spot.

They nuzzled me, sniffed my hair, lay their heads on my shoulder, and were quite protective of me. When the colt got a little too frisky, prancing and kicking up her heels, the "King of the Hill," Yum-Yum, a handsome gelding, stood between her and me.

One time a board on the fence broke as I was climbing over, and I fell to the ground. I lay there a few moments, stunned, only to feel a gentle nudging at the top of my head. It was Yum-Yum, seeing if I was all right.

As I picked blackberries, they were close on my heels, trying to eat out of my bucket and following me everywhere, even if they *knew* I didn't have food.

Yum-Yum especially seemed to reflect my own mood. If I were upset or crying, he came close and put his head down, a sign of submission from my equine friend.

Sometimes we all played in the water, splashing in the pond, and I taught them to drink out of a hose. I occasionally had to scold one or the other for something minor.

Although there was some degree of allergy, it was minimal, especially in comparison to what I had experienced in the past. I thought it a miracle since I now liked the horses almost better than I liked Johnny. I had the feeling that the relationship had run its course and was dying a natural death, although we were still the best of friends.

From time to time, I have heard of therapy horses, helpful in treating children with autism to angry adolescents, providing physical and psychological benefits. Although I never really learned to ride, the incredible bond that I felt with these powerful animals provided the best kind of therapy for me and was exactly what I needed at that time in my life.

I have now come to believe in "little miracles." These are the things that happen every day that sometimes go unnoticed and unappreciated. I think we have come to expect drama from our miracles, but a flower, a kindness or a good friend can all be miracles, especially if that "good friend" is 16 hands high, weighs a thousand pounds and eats hay.

A reason, a season or a lifetime? Altogether, my time with Johnny and the horses allowed me to share, grow, heal and learn, but the season was over.

Chapter 21

Cruisin'

The other side of loneliness
The other side of the blues
There really is a place like this
Where the sun is gonna shine for you
You'll feel that old restlessness
Your tears have all been cried
You'll find your way over this
And you'll make it to the other side

-The Other Side, Wynona Judd

Eventually, I was able to summon the strength needed to put Johnny in the past and move on. The empty spot in my heart where he had once been became only a shadow, and I was sure it would disappear completely with time. It always had before, and my faith was strong. In my heart, I now truly wished him well.

Perhaps more importantly, I had felt God's quiet presence on Johnny's farm. Now I prayed to find it again.

I was able to focus, as usual, by concentrating on my job. At some point, things came to a head with my supervisor and I decided I had no choice but to leave.

No one had ever questioned my professionalism, dedication or competence until now. I knew in my heart that I had done well in spite of having to work around my few remaining cognitive problems.

In the past, I had dealt with out-of-control show business egos, worried business owners and temperamental divas. Never had I had a problem getting along with anyone and I had a tendency to take way too much abuse.

A dressing down from my supervisor for taking a business phone call at home became the last straw for someone who had specifically requested flexibility in the position in the first place.

Professionalism is not necessarily a 9-to-5 concept, and most workaholics incorporate their life into their work and their work into their life. This enables a person to become "married to the job" and give 110 percent, not always a good thing, but it was how I functioned best. I didn't really have a life outside of work.

I knew that I could probably make more money and have a lot more self-respect elsewhere. I could even start my own business again. I wasn't sure where I would go or what I would do, I just knew I couldn't stay there any longer and gave notice.

My young co-worker had continued to harass and display open hostility toward me as well as to Marcy, our easygoing and personable administrative assistant, with whom I got along well. But that week, surprisingly, she tried to instigate peace talks between my supervisor and me.

To her credit, my boss, had the skill and courage to turn a negative into a positive and to work through whatever personal differences there may have been, allowing us to form a more cohesive team. In the end, I agreed to stay.

Eventually, a somewhat fragile and inconsistent but workable spirit of camaraderie developed among our staff of four, which contributed to our successes, and the Nashville UAW-Ford Center built a reputation for creative, innovative programming that other centers replicated.

My supervisor eventually left, another company took over the contract, and I ended up staying with the program for more than four years.

My experience there gave me a glimpse into the fascinating world of automobile manufacturing, unions, negotiations, a pattern of employment and a way of life that seems to be disappearing. I saw how the union and management interacted to solve problems and build business. Within our local union chapter and the plant we served, there was a spirit of complete cooperation.

I saw how the fortunes of a global company affected the worker's daily lives. I discovered a corporate culture of loyal, happy employees and retirees, many of whom had been with the company for nearly forty years.

Drawing on my knowledge of filmmaking, I even made a documentary framing this culture and preserving it for posterity as well as for my own memories. Many of these people had become more than friends; they had become my "family." They brought me gifts, came to my housewarming party, and we celebrated holidays together. I attended their family functions, including birthday parties and, sadly, funerals.

Their unwavering love, support and acceptance helped heal my heart, as well as my mind. This was also the first time I truly felt financially secure.

I was still occasionally making music, eventually spending time in a nearby recording studio and had fallen in with a group of Nashville songwriters, so I always felt creatively challenged and stayed busy.

I traveled to Memphis to see Brian and helped him get a house there. Mom and Dad came to visit and I took them to Monell's, a favorite Nashville restaurant that serves food at long tables, family style. At the beginning of the meal, you might be eating with strangers but by dessert, you've made new friends. Dad jokingly tried to tell our tablemates that he was country star Porter Wagoner but they didn't buy it.

Leaving work in the evening to a beautiful sunset on the West side of Music City, U.S.A., I counted my blessings daily. I appreciated the focus of the program in Nashville as well as the benefits that came with the job. This was the first time I'd had any work related perks of note. While in their employ, in 2004, I went on my first real vacation.

I hadn't seen my buddy Rachelle in over 12 years, although we had maintained intermittent contact and the friendship was as strong as ever. Sharon, who had worked with me at the clinic and even lived with Rachelle and me for a short time, had visited when she came to Tennessee to see her son. For my first real vacation, Rachelle, Sharon and I went to Florida and from there, embarked on a Caribbean cruise Rachelle had won.

In spite of my travels, I had never been to Florida before. I knew I loved the Wild West and East Tennessee, but I expected a bug-infested, alligator-laden, sauna-like environment filled only with people over age 80. The draw for me was getting to be with my friends once again. Together we explored Fort Lauderdale, Pompano Beach and the Bahamas.

What I found in Florida that March was a tropical paradise with lush foliage, interesting inhabitants and great food. And the food was even better on the cruise ship. I ate my way from Miami to Nassau and back again!

I was particularly taken with the white sand, blue water and history of Nassau. Sharon was particularly taken with the casino at the Atlantis Resort. Rachelle had won the vacation package but it was she who spent much of the cruise in a Dramamine-induced sleep… seasick.

Our friendship was such that it allowed for individuality and autonomy. We each did whatever we felt like in any situation while still being a support and sounding board for the others. This allowed us to pursue our own interests separately, onboard and in the ports of call.

Later we reported new friendships made on deck and compared notes on food. We tried to take advantage of each and every activity onboard and giggled like schoolgirls as we planned our days. We had pretend fights over the bathroom and understood when quiet time was needed.

Lying high on a secluded deck watching the sun set across the waves, the three of us talked and the years fell away like needles off last season's Christmas tree. With all of our children now grown, we had covered so much ground. It was a reality check for friends who had undergone adversity and change: a reunion of the comrades. We were able to relax and enjoy the whole experience and planned to do it again.

In 2005, we all cruised to Key West and Cozumel, taking Rachelle's mother. When Rachelle and Sharon went off in search of ancient ruins, I went to McDonald's. Later, upon reflection, I wondered why I had gone to Mexico to eat at a McDonald's, then come home and immediately gone to the local neighborhood Mexican restaurant. I hoped there would be a next time so I could get it right.

Both cruises were relaxing and rewarding. I came home invigorated, happy and feeling great.

I remembered feeling like this at the top of the Ferris wheel in Ventura, Calif., when Brian was young and also while driving through the rugged terrain of Utah on band trips. I was more content than I had ever been, getting together with my dear friends. I wondered what had become of my other college friend from Utah, Penny.

The days flew by and I felt good about life in general. I loved my job in Nashville.

I had learned to deal with my limitations in many ways but preferred to focus on the things I *could* do - my strengths. This eventually proved invaluable in building a business as well as counseling others. My common sense, grass roots approach was the only avenue available to me and was helpful to others needing to get back on track. Sometimes businesses as well as individuals need to refocus on the things they do best.

Romance was no longer a part of my life because I tended to take people at their word, not always a wise choice in the world of dating. I also felt that I had invested so much of myself in Johnny that I didn't have much left to give.

But I made many friends because I had learned to relate to people from a very real, positive place within the heart. Sharing of myself willingly and openly, I'm gut-wrenchingly honest. I can't be any other way. Unfortunately, I can't take credit for this, I simply don't have the ability to be false or play games any more. My smile is genuine.

Only rarely now did I think about the brain injury or the long years of recovery. I thought often of my former customers and friends on the rose route and felt that time in my life had been a valuable bridge to where I was now. I had come a long way. I had renewed connections. Even old memories were starting to come back.

In the mid-eighties, working as an activity director at a convalescent center in Salt Lake, I had come across a small, battery-powered instrument called an Omnichord at a yard sale. Taking it to work with me, I let the residents play it.

Miss Nellie, bedridden and completely unresponsive, was not a part of the group that played cards or games. She rarely spoke or even opened her eyes. She was still alive, but barely.

On a whim one day, I was leaving with my little instrument in hand and stopped by her room. Her eyes were shut, and she was as quiet and still as usual. Sitting in a chair, I began softly playing and singing some of the old gospel hymns Dad had taught me.

After about 10 minutes, I left. I did this several more times on the spur of the moment, in all honesty more for me than for her. She never responded in any way.

One day, I had just come out of her room with my instrument and gone to the common area when I heard commotion. An aide came running from her direction. Hearing her name and seeing the excitement, I thought it was a Code Blue and that Miss Nellie had died. Maybe my singing had killed her.

As I and others rushed into her room, there she lay, eyes closed and still as ever, softly singing, word for word *In the Sweet Bye and Bye*, one of the songs I'd sung to her moments earlier.

This instrument came out of the mothballs after the brain injury and I credit it with helping me to regain the use of my right hand and fingers.

In my new job at Ford, one of our volunteer projects was singing at local nursing homes and assisted living facilities. I became the leader of this small group and once again rescued the little music machine from the back of my closet. It was now missing buttons, scratched and scuffed, but still working. Some of the places we visited didn't have pianos so it came in very handy.

The activity directors at several of the centers were overwhelmed with curiosity about my little portable music maker and wondered where they could get something like that, so I did a little research.

The Omnichord had been redesigned and redefined into the QChord, and now included attachments, cases and accessories. Establishing contact with the company, I chatted with them about marketing to physical therapists, recreational therapists, activity coordinators and the elderly. I already knew its potential.

One of the directors told me there was going to be a national convention for activity professionals in Gatlinburg, near Knoxville, my old stomping ground, and I should try to demonstrate this instrument that virtually anyone could learn to play.

Through a series of convenient coincidences, I was able to take time off and go to the show as a commercial vendor, showing the QChord at my own booth. Thursday evening at the hotel, I set up and distributed flyers. Friday morning, as I headed downstairs, I heard a once familiar voice call, "CARLA!?"

I hadn't been Carla in years. Startled, I turned to see Penny, my old buddy from Utah. She had eventually finished her degree and was now working as an activity coordinator in Arizona. Through tears and hugs, we picked up where we left off, 18 years later.

Surrounded by the Great Smoky Mountains, we filled each other in on our children's activities and professional lives and reminisced about old times, vowing never to lose contact again.

The next year I was scheduled to offer two short workshops on other subjects at a conference for the same organization in Scottsdale, Ariz.

Once again, Penny and I met, took a day off to catch up and again vowed not to lose touch. We ran off to explore the state with its deserts, cactus and cowboys as only two middle-aged, fun-loving women could.

Sitting in a chapel, high above the magical beauty of Sedona, a quiet peace gripped us both as an unspoken communication between friends became almost tangible. With utter clarity, I saw how important the female friendships had been in my life and felt complete gratitude for the little woman sitting next to me as well as for Rachelle, Sharon, Jo Ann and the others who had befriended me. I realized that each of our lives had been a patchwork quilt of experiences, good and bad and similar. And although we had not maintained relationships on a regular basis, I knew that no matter how much time passed, the one thing I could count on would be that unique bond of sisterhood and friendship.

I also knew with certainty that there was a reason for everything, as the crazy pieces of my life fell into place in the shadow of the red rocks and the quiet of the desert.

In the fall of 2005, flying into the Detroit airport, I was happy and content as I met with others for job-related training. The only fly in the ointment was my still-antagonistic co-worker back in Nashville who was now openly critical of everything having to do with our programs, as well as our character and personal qualities.

Since our supervisor left, she was no longer the teachers pet and there was no one to diffuse her emotional highs and lows or assuage her intense insecurities. She found fault with our activities, our participants and even with the prizes I gathered for monthly Bingo games! She seemed to especially resent my very presence.

Chapter 22

Beale Street & Bar-B-Q

I can see clearly now, the rain is gone,
I can see all obstacles in my way
Gone are the dark clouds that had me blind
It's gonna be a bright, bright
Sunshiny day.

- I can See Clearly Now, Johnny Nash

As an adult, I have tried to live by the philosophy that if you can't say something nice, don't say anything at all. If I must weigh in on something or offer an opinion, I try to offer it tactfully and from a constructive, positive point of view. Diplomacy has been a hallmark of successful people, and I have found it especially helpful in business situations.

However, if I said something was black, my co-worker would say it was white. If I said day, she said night. If I liked something, she was automatically against it. Her criticisms were often unfounded, harsh and stinging.

Although Marcy was not immune and was occasionally a target, even she was shocked at the blatant display of contempt this woman held for me, and we warned each other of our volatile colleague's mood each morning when we came in for the day.

We were temporary contract players in a big-time environment and didn't want to make waves or cause problems, so we said little. Our new supervisor, in Norfolk, Va., was in charge of several centers at different geographic locations. Although she was sympathetic to our plight and frustrated with our co-worker as well, there was little she could do from a remote location to stay on top of things daily, although she tried.

Constantly tiptoeing around on eggshells because of someone's frame of mind was not my idea of a professional environment, nor could I function well under such a cloud of pettiness and negativity.

Finally, it got to a point where neither Marcy nor I particularly wanted to interact with our prickly coworker. Her cynical, sarcastic and increasingly hostile barbs were now even aimed at the company for which we worked, but I was always her favorite target.

Once again, after four years with UAW-Ford, I decided to leave and was about to give notice. Helping to host an event at work, I was walking down the hallway with several of our regular female participants. My co-worker made yet another snide, condescending and degrading remark directed at me and walked away.

Normally, I would have seen it coming and redirected the onlookers' attention, interrupted her, made light of it or changed the subject before she finished. I didn't want the people we served to feel uncomfortable, like they had been caught up in a petty catfight or that they had to choose between us.

This time, however, I was through protecting her and just stood there.

Her attitude spoke for itself. The participants, whom I thought of as dear friends, stood in shocked disbelief with their mouths open and eyes wide.

One of them finally said, "How long has that been going on?"

"Since Day one," I answered truthfully.

"We *thought* we heard her making rude comments about you before, but we just couldn't believe it." said the other.

"Are *you* gonna *take* that?" asked the first one.

"Aw, what can I do?" I asked.

"Well, I would have decked her - I just about *did*! I can't believe she just did that."

My friends were not exactly timid, shy or retiring, and I was both amused and touched that they were upset on my behalf. I knew I was leaving by then, and these women now knew why. Apparently others had overheard comments between my former boss and this co-worker concerning me in the past and already suspected why I was leaving.

They and others, as well as the company, tried to get me to stay, but eventually Marcy and I left at the same time. I encouraged our participants to continue to take advantage of the programs offered, many of which I'd helped initiate. Marcy moved to Chattanooga to be with family and I moved to Memphis, then back to East Tennessee to my beloved mountains. Marcy and I remain friends yet.

I still hear from my UAW-Ford family and they, like the hard-scrabble folks on my rose route, will always be a part of me. As a long-time employee stated in the film I produced, my blood still runs "Ford Blue."

In Memphis, I spent steamy nights on my front porch listening to live blues from Central Bar-B-Q wafting through the neighborhood. The air was heavy with the aroma of food mixed with the sweet smell of summer blossoms.

I have memories of friendly people, graceful Southern architecture and fantastic gardens, the Mississippi River, wonderful residents at the huge retirement community where I worked, and most of all, the cherished infant grandson I now had.

Mason looked exactly like Brian did at that tender age, and I treasured every moment I could spend with him.

Unfortunately, things had not worked out between my son and Mason's mother, and Brian had moved back to Knoxville. I was taking over his small house in Midtown, but my primary reason for moving to the home of Beale Street and Elvis was because Mason lived nearby. However, I worked long hours as an activity director and didn't get to see him nearly as much as I wanted.

I tried to adjust to my new home but when I wasn't working I spent a lot of time alone. Memphis was unlike any other place I had ever been and in spite of its unique charm, it felt strange. I missed Nashville and even more, I missed the mountains and the homegrown spirit of East Tennessee.

Still, I persevered. I liked my job, fixed up the house and began to investigate the attractions of the city. There were great restaurants, art galleries, parks and a fantastic zoo.

While attending a concert by Ladysmith Black Mambazo at a large church, their soft African acapella harmonies lulled me into a peaceful, comtemplative reverie. I was aware of how much I had changed over the years and had developed a deep appreciation for life, for different cultures and a sense of acceptance - of myself as well as others.

Had I accepted my new life here? Was Memphis where I wanted to spend the rest of my days? There were indications that I was needed by family and business matters back in East Tennessee and I had no one here – except Mason. I was still very lonely, something I had never felt in the mountains of East Tennessee even when I was alone.

West Tennessee was like a different world, and I didn't feel quite at home.

Indecision became my most frequent companion.

Somewhat reluctantly, I finally put the house up for sale and began making preparations to move, once again.

That same week, a classical guitarist originally from Puerto Rico was scheduled to perform at work.

As I walked into the lobby, meeting him for the first time, our eyes locked and for the first time in a long while, I felt a spark of chemistry. Openly and unabashedly flirting (to the amusement of the residents), we exchanged phone numbers, then talked on the phone regularly.

Three weeks later, I went to the restaurant where he was performing. The next night, we went out to eat and the following night, he came to my house where we talked into the night, he in his broken English and I in my Wisconsin-Hillbilly patois.

Javier, close to my age and a perfect gentleman, was graduating from the University of Memphis with a master's degree and was undecided about what to do next. I could offer no encouragement one way or the other because I felt that my future, too, was up in the air.

Our kisses bore a stamp of tentative innocence because it had been a while since either of us had kissed anyone. I wasn't sure I remembered how, and wasn't sure I had any business kissing anyone at age 52. Didn't I have better things to do? No.

Proceeding with caution but never fully consummating the affair, for the first time in years I felt like a desirable woman.

We skirted around the issue of a future together like a game of cat and mouse, hinting at maybe even staying in Memphis, but my house was sold by now, and I'd given my 30-day notice at work.

In the end, the tentative relationship was curtailed due to the uncertainty of both of our lives. We did become fast friends as we both made plans to leave - he to pursue opportunities in Arizona and I, back to East Tennessee. But our final days in Memphis were happy and fun-filled, though colored with thoughts of what could have been.

Back in Pigeon Forge, a tourist area near the Great Smoky Mountains, I became involved in the entertainment industry once again and began performing with the Patty Waszak Show. In 2006 I entered the Tennessee Country Music Association competition where I won the Rising Star Female Vocalist of the Year, Most Promising Female Entertainer of the Year and Clogger of the Year awards. Not bad for someone who couldn't have stuttered her way through the title of a song, if she could have remembered it, 10 years before.

Progress had come to me slowly. Time, patience, experience and education had allowed me objectivity toward my own life and many wounds had healed. My intellectual capabilities in some respects were greater than they ever were although there was still a lot I could not do. Still, I was learning lessons that I perhaps could not have learned any other way.

Johnny and the horses taught me courage, patience and how to play again.

Victoria's family and the house on Highland Avenue gave me respite and security.

My friends at Ford taught me loyalty, strength and true friendship.

The rose route taught me to trust and have faith.

I feel now that the negative baggage I had been carrying around previously prevented me from acquiring these things in a meaningful sense before. These were gifts that a higher power possibly couldn't have bestowed without literally knocking me in the head.

From my perspective now, I can indeed see that *everything* has a purpose.

Things do happen for a reason, and there is usually a lesson if we will open ourselves up to learning. Unfortunately, many of us must unlearn a great deal before we can take that next step.

Chapter 23

Moving On...

And if the night runs over
And if the day won't last
And if your way should falter
Along this stony pass

It's just a moment
This time will pass

- Stuck in a Moment, Bono, U2

As I continue on my journey through life, there have been and will continue to be trials and tests as well as victories and happiness and I occasionally take time to marvel at how the story is turning out so far.

My parents have mellowed through the years, become my best friends and celebrated their 61st anniversary. In spite of our ups and downs, they have been my staunchest supporters. Loving family ties remain strong.

I go home to Wisconsin now, and we pile into the car, traipsing around the countryside, me in search of restaurants that serve cheese curds, Dad driving cautiously and Mom riding shotgun. At their house, we look through old albums at black and white photographs of my grandparents and great-grandparents, long-lost aunts and uncles, and faces I don't even know.

We visit the cemetery in Albion and I hear the echoes of a long ago childhood and fight off mosquitos amid the ancient pines.

I find remnants of later years in Janesville where the General Motors plant, once the lifeblood of the community, is now silent. I run into Gary, the drummer for my first band. Tumbleweed Rock's glory days are long gone, but the bond of close friendship is still there.

I see my first husband, now remarried. We smile but don't really speak. The warmth in his eyes says more than words ever could.

My brother Clark and his wife invite me over to watch a movie, I catch up with my nephew Richard and go out on the town with my childhood friend, Jo Ann.

Brian has grown into a kind and intelligent man with his own story to tell. He lives in Knoxville now with his two cats. Mason still lives near Memphis.

Rachelle has been certified as a nurse practitioner and works with the Veteran's Administration. Although we're miles apart, the closeness and understanding are still there.

Penny is still in Arizona.

I don't see Johnny much anymore, but I hear from him every now and then. About relationships, he says he's like a dog chasing a car – he doesn't know what to do with it once he catches it. The horses live with his nephew in North Carolina.

Sometimes I can still sense Lynn around me but believe that he may finally be at peace. In the manner of a battle-weary soldier, he once told me pain was our friend. It lets us know we're alive. I think he meant physical pain, but the same could be said of emotional pain as well.

Joy also lets us experience life to its fullest and I make a conscious decision each day to be happy and appreciate life.

Looking back, it seems that there were many tears, but maybe it's just that we remember the sorrows more vividly than the joys in life. And maybe that's something we can consciously change. At the risk of sounding cliche, it takes sun and rain to make rainbows.

I have changed much, but in doing so I know that whatever comes, I can handle it.

It's been 16 years since the head injury. I don't have regular headaches any more, but I continue to have occasional vision, hearing and some neurological-based issues. There are sometimes gaps in my memory, and I still have certain cognitive problems. All of this seems inconsequential though. I'm alive.

I no longer feel the need for approval or applause and do not seek validation any longer. My self-worth now comes from within. Humor has become an important ally, as has spirituality.

Small talk still does not come as easily to me as it once did. Then again, most of my inhibitions are gone, imparting a newfound sense of freedom and a creative license that often accompanies a removal of limitations.

In the past, I may have been held back by a vague self-consciousness, worry about what others would think and subliminal thoughts of censure and repression. It has been replaced with simple joy.

Confidence in the business world has come from that joy as well and from knowing and building on my strengths.

Even mild TBI can result in some marked personality changes. Some victims have become more short-tempered and aggressive. Others become calmer and more docile. It has been noted that many adults with head injuries seem to possess a more childlike point of view - they develop a more candid nature, lack of guile and pretentiousness. This can be unnerving or refreshing, depending on the situation. Sometimes there is a spontaneous glee and impish sense of humor. It's almost as if a layer of shallowness has been stripped away and I wonder if I'm perceived in that way.

The brain is a remarkable organ, powerful and complex. Injuries and recovery are unpredictable at best. As science learns more, perhaps greater inroads will be made toward treating brain-related injuries and their complications, but right now prevention is the only antidote.

I tell people to use seat belts, wear helmets, observe safety rules - and don't sit under television sets.

Others have experienced far more hardship and drama in their lives, and I am in awe of their spirit and courage. I have made some poor choices and decisions, as we all do, and for those I accept responsibility. I have learned from my mistakes. I am human. I have also forgiven myself.

Early in life I confronted the Almighty, crying, "Why me?" in anguish or in tears, at the situations and circumstances in which I found myself – some of my own making. Often, unfolding events have felt much like a board game where the roll of the dice or spin of an arrow dictated whether I took a step forward or two backward.

I've sometimes had the feeling that my life was out of control and obviously, some things are indeed out of our control.

Perhaps accepting that fact and learning to control what we *can* may be a key to happiness.

I now ask, "Why me?" with awe and wonder, looking at things in an entirely different light. Why was I singled out for the unique and often difficult challenges that allowed me to grow and learn and develop strength, empathy and understanding?

I have realized in retrospect that the hardships may have truly been blessings in disguise. The broad and colorful tapestry of my life has been woven with lessons I needed to learn.

I have discovered the truth in the old adage that it's not whether you win or lose, but how you play the game that matters. I am no longer as concerned with the destination as I am with the journey and have learned to appreciate today.

These days, I entertain occasionally with shows in the Pigeon Forge area near the Smoky Mountains. Sometimes I perform as one of the area's most famous citizens, Dolly Parton. Other times, I appear as 'Tweedy,' a lively character in curlers and bathrobe, with horn-rimmed glasses askew and toting a plunger. And often, I appear as myself.

I occasionally attend doctoral level classes at the nearby University of Tennessee, in case the show-biz thing doesn't work out and in the never-ending quest for knowledge. I have good friends, a training and development business and a home filled with peace - a refuge for recharging my batteries. In short, I have much for which to be thankful.

Sitting with my friend Penny, surrounded by the Tennessee hills I visited as a child, I felt I had completed a full circle in more ways than one. I now have favorite spots within the National Park that I visit often to reflect on life and to be one with nature and God.

The sense of restlessness that I felt for so many years is no longer there. Did that come from maturity? Have I finally grown comfortable with who and what I am? Or am I just where I'm supposed to be?

Maybe both.

The peace I have always sought in these friendly mountains, my father's ancestral roots, is not within the hills themselves, but within myself and my Creator. Although I feel most comfortable here, I know that I could be happy anywhere because true happiness lies within the spirit, not in the place. Still, the place puts me in touch with the spirit. Maybe some were born to dwell here.

In the Smoky Mountains, one can still hear the gentle whisper of a mountain breeze and feel the power of nature in the soft, rolling thunder of the hills. The tree-covered slopes are old and the echoes of time have not diminished their unique character and history.

It is my history, and I carry a piece of it with me always.

Epilogue

Long Hard Winter...

I'm starting with the man in the mirror
I'm asking him to change his ways
And no message could have been any clearer
If you wanna make the world a better place
Take a look at yourself and then make a change

- Man in the Mirror, Michael Jackson

It was originally suggested that I write about my experience with traumatic brain injury, but I found that I couldn't write about a life-changing event without writing about the life, so it has included much more than I ever intended. Still, I've left out many people and experiences that helped shape me.

I've omitted the kindness of friends and neighbors and the heartlessness of others. Not mentioned are other celebrities I've met, accidents, arrests, whether or not I thought O.J. was guilty and so very much more.

Looking back, I see three main themes running through my life, No. 1 being perseverance. I have hung in there. I plodded on. Sometimes I didn't know where I was going, but I persevered. It may have been the wrong path, but I persevered. My efforts may not have always paid off but I persevered.

Dad once compared me to the Energizer bunny, a stuffed rabbit from an ad campaign who never stops walking and drumming a big drum due to his wonderful, long-lasting batteries. My batteries may have been low at certain points, but I kept walking and drumming. Sometimes all we can do is muddle on and do the next thing.

What kept me from giving up at times was the second theme: hope. Hope is what keeps our dreams alive and gets us out of bed in the morning. Hope may shine like a beacon at times and be only a dull glow from an ember at others, but it is there even if sometimes you must look hard to find it. There *is* always hope - for the future, for a better life, for joy, for faith…I learned to live with hope in my heart.

The last theme is change. It's inevitable.

Legendary rhythm and blues singer/songwriter Sam Cooke sings,

"It's been a long, a long time coming, but I know a change gon' come, oh yes it will."

And it will. Maybe that's the one thing we can count on.

Many of us don't like change because it is often forced upon us. Sometimes change happens so fast that we can't keep up with it. Sometimes we fight change because we think we may not like where it is leading.

Yes, change is often out of our control, but our attitude, our thoughts, our actions and how we deal with change *are* under our control.

Maybe you can't change life, circumstances or those around you, but you can change yourself. In fact, sometimes the only true change you can make is from within.

Long Hard Winter

C.J. Morgan

Time is spent, lessons in the learning
Each summertime is followed by the fall
Things are as they should be
And I open my eyes to the call.

In good times and bad, there is comfort,
In every life a little rain must fall,
Every storm that passes makes you stronger
Soon you realize you've weathered them all.

Chorus: And it's gonna be a long, hard winter
And it's gonna be a late, wet spring
But maybe by the time summer rolls around once again,
My heart and soul, they will sing, my heart and soul will sing.

The seasons of my grief are almost over
The wintry winds of loneliness almost gone
I'm feeling my way through the darkest of night
Slowly making my way toward dawn.

I thank God for the long hard winters
With the frozen ground at rest
With its solitude and comfort
I am truly, richly blessed.
Repeat chorus

About the Author

C.J. Morgan has been a performer, public relations consultant, trainer and more. With a BS in Communication from the University of Utah and a masters degree in Educational Psychology from the University of Tennessee, she develops workshops on a broad array of subjects and is available to speak at your conference, convention or event. Visit www.cjmorgantraining.com or call 615-289-4815 for more information

For more copies of this book, please send check or money order made out to *Tennessee Roselady* for $24.95, plus $5.99 per book for shipping and handling to:

Top Ten Productions
P.O. Box 6904
Sevierville, TN 37894-6904
or visit
www. www.tnroselady.com

LaVergne, TN USA
22 November 2009
164991LV00004B/2/P